To the insatiable minds and the voracious explorers.

Here's to the lifelong learners, who reveal the beauty

that lies in embracing the adventure just as much as

the final outcome.

Table of Contents

ACCOUNTANT

An accountant is like a detective who investigates how much money a company or individual makes and spends. They also help people make smart financial decisions.

Imagine that you want to start your own candy store. You'll need to buy ingredients, make the candy, and sell it to customers. But how do you know if your store is making money? That's where an accountant comes in. They keep track of the amount of money you spend on ingredients, equipment, and rent. They also keep track of how much money you make by selling candy. By subtracting the expenses from the income, they can tell you if your store is profitable.

An accountant can also help you make good decisions about how to spend your money. For example, if you want to buy a new candy-making machine, an accountant can help you figure out if it's a smart investment. They'll look at how much money you're currently making and how much more candy you could produce with the new machine. Then they'll help you decide if the cost of the machine is worth it.

But accounting isn't just about numbers. Accountants also need to be good problem solvers. For example, imagine that your candy store accidentally made too much candy for a big event and now you have a lot of extra inventory. An accountant can help you figure out what to do with it. They might suggest having a sale to get rid of the extra candy or donating it to a charity.

Another important part of accounting is making sure that all the numbers are accurate. It is important because if the numbers are wrong, it can cause big problems for a business or individual.

In addition to helping businesses and individuals, accountants also play an important role in society. They help ensure that everyone pays the right amount of taxes and that government agencies have accurate financial records. Without accountants, it would be much harder to keep track of all the money in the world!

So, if you're good with numbers, like solving problems, and want to help people make smart financial decisions, accounting might be the job for you. Whether you want to start your own candy store or work for a big accounting firm, there are many different opportunities for accountants. And who knows, maybe one day you'll be the one helping others keep track of their money and make smart financial decisions!

ACTOR / ACTRESS

An actor or actress is a creative chameleon, possessing the extraordinary ability to bring stories to life and captivate audiences by embodying a diverse range of characters. They are the artists who transport us to different worlds, evoke powerful emotions, and inspire us through their compelling performances.

Imagine stepping onto a Broadway stage, breathing life into a beloved character from a classic play, or starring in a critically acclaimed film that touches the hearts of millions. As an actor or actress, you'll hone your craft through training and experience, embracing diverse roles across theater, film, television, and even voice-over work for animation and video games.

The journey to becoming an accomplished actor or actress often begins with formal training at a drama school or conservatory, where you'll learn the fundamentals of acting, voice, movement, and character development. You may also participate in workshops and masterclasses to further sharpen your skills and explore specific acting techniques.

An actor's career is often marked by auditions, an essential process where you'll showcase your talent and suitability for a role. Networking is also a vital component of success in this industry, as building relationships with fellow actors, directors, casting agents, and other industry professionals can open doors to new opportunities.

Success in acting may be measured in different ways, from landing a steady stream of roles to earning recognition from peers and critics through awards and accolades. Think of Meryl Streep's versatile performances, earning her numerous Academy Award nominations, or Tom Hanks' unforgettable portrayals in films like "Forrest Gump" and "Cast Away."

Actors and actresses often find themselves in unique and exciting situations, such as performing in exotic locations, working with renowned directors, or sharing the screen with talented co-stars. While the acting profession is filled with glamour and excitement, it's essential to acknowledge the challenges that come with it. Competition is fierce, and finding steady work can be difficult, with periods of unemployment being common. Actors often need to supplement their income with other jobs while waiting for their big break. Resilience and determination are key qualities to succeed in this field.

ACTUARY

An actuary is a master of calculated risk, possessing the uncanny ability to peer into the future and predict the likelihood of events that could impact individuals, businesses, and societies. They are the analytical wizards who use mathematics, statistics, and financial theory to assess and manage risk in industries such as insurance, finance, and pensions.

Imagine being the numerical genius who designs an innovative insurance policy that protects a cutting-edge space tourism company or develops a pension plan that provides financial security for thousands of retirees. As an actuary, you'll play a critical role in shaping financial strategies, ensuring that organizations are prepared to face uncertainty.

Actuaries often work in insurance companies, analyzing data to calculate the probability of accidents, illnesses, natural disasters, and other events that may lead to financial losses. For instance, they may use historical data to predict the likelihood of a hurricane striking a coastal region, helping insurance companies set appropriate premiums and establish adequate reserves to cover potential claims.

In the world of finance, actuaries contribute their expertise to investment strategies, risk management, and financial product development. They might create a new financial instrument that allows investors to hedge against fluctuations in currency exchange rates or assess the risk exposure of a company's investment portfolio.

Pensions and retirement planning are also key areas where actuaries make a significant impact. They analyze demographic data and economic trends to design pension plans that balance benefits for retirees with the long-term financial stability of the fund. In this capacity, they help ensure that retirees can enjoy a secure and comfortable retirement.

Actuaries typically have a strong background in mathematics and often hold degrees in fields like actuarial science, statistics, or mathematics. A successful actuary possesses not only exceptional analytical skills but also the ability to communicate complex concepts to non-experts. They must present their findings and recommendations to decision-makers, translating data-driven insights into actionable strategies.

The demand for actuaries is on the rise, thanks to the increasing complexity of the financial landscape and the growing need for risk management expertise. This translates to excellent job prospects and competitive salaries for those who choose this career path.

ADVERTISING EXECUTIVE

Advertising executives are the people who come up with cool and creative ideas to help companies sell their products and services. They are the imaginative masterminds who fuse art and commerce, crafting persuasive messages that inspire action and fuel the success of businesses and organizations.

Picture yourself working with a team of talented creatives, devising an unforgettable Super Bowl ad that captures the hearts and minds of millions or launching a viral social media campaign that sparks a global conversation. As an advertising executive, you'll navigate the dynamic world of marketing, exploring new ways to connect with audiences and leave a lasting impression.

Advertising executives work closely with clients to identify their marketing objectives and target audiences. They then develop comprehensive advertising strategies that align with these goals, incorporating a mix of traditional and digital media channels to maximize reach and impact. For example, they might blend eye-catching billboards, engaging TV commercials, and clever social media content to promote a new product.

In this role, you'll collaborate with a diverse team of professionals, including copywriters, graphic designers, media planners, and account managers, to bring your campaigns to life. You'll oversee the creative process from concept to execution, ensuring that each element of the campaign adheres to the client's vision and brand identity.

An example of an impactful advertising campaign is the "Share a Coke" initiative by Coca-Cola, which featured personalized bottles with common names and phrases. This innovative strategy not only boosted sales but also fostered a sense of connection among consumers, demonstrating the power of effective advertising.

To succeed as an advertising executive, you'll need a diverse skill set that includes creativity, strategic thinking, project management, and communication. A background in marketing, advertising, or communications is often beneficial, and many professionals in the field hold degrees in these disciplines.

The advertising industry is constantly evolving, with new technologies and platforms offering fresh opportunities for innovation and engagement. As an advertising executive, you'll need to stay abreast of emerging trends and adapt your strategies accordingly. This environment presents exciting challenges and the chance to continually learn and grow.

AERODYNAMICIST

An aerodynamicist is an engineer who specializes in the study of the motion of air and its interaction with solid objects, such as aircraft, cars, and buildings. These professionals play a pivotal role in designing, testing, and optimizing the performance of various structures and vehicles, contributing to their efficiency, safety, and sustainability.

Aerodynamicists are often tasked with analyzing and solving complex fluid dynamics problems. They employ advanced mathematical models, computational tools, and experimental techniques to assess and enhance the aerodynamic properties of various designs. By doing so, they seek to minimize air resistance, reduce drag, and improve overall performance.

In the realm of aviation, aerodynamicists work on the design and optimization of aircraft, from commercial airliners to military jets and drones. They collaborate with multidisciplinary teams to develop efficient airframes, wings, and control surfaces that ensure stability, maneuverability, and fuel efficiency. They also contribute to the development of innovative propulsion systems and materials, striving to reduce the environmental impact of air travel.

The automotive industry also relies on the expertise of aerodynamicists. They help design and refine the shapes of cars, trucks, and motorcycles to improve fuel efficiency, handling, and top speed. This is accomplished through wind tunnel testing, computational fluid dynamics simulations (CFD), and on-road experiments. In motorsports, such as Formula 1 and NASCAR, aerodynamicists play a critical role in the quest for a competitive edge, optimizing vehicle designs to balance speed, handling, and stability.

Beyond transportation, aerodynamicists contribute to the design of energy-efficient buildings and infrastructure. They analyze the impact of wind on structures and provide insights into how to minimize turbulence, optimize ventilation, and harness wind energy using turbines. They also collaborate on the development of wind farms, optimizing the layout and design of turbines to maximize power generation.

To become an aerodynamicist, one typically pursues a bachelor's degree in aerospace engineering, mechanical engineering, or a related field. Advanced positions may require a master's or doctoral degree, with specialized coursework in fluid dynamics, aerodynamics, and computational methods.

AGRICULTURIST

An agriculturist is a professional who focuses on the cultivation and management of crops, livestock, and other resources to optimize agricultural production. These experts play a critical role in ensuring food security, promoting sustainable farming practices, and contributing to the overall well-being of the global population.

Agriculturists have a deep understanding of plant and animal sciences, soil management, and modern farming techniques. They apply this knowledge to enhance crop yields, improve animal health and welfare, and optimize the use of resources such as land, water, and fertilizers.

In crop production, agriculturists study plant genetics, breeding, and nutrition to develop high-yielding, disease-resistant, and climate-resilient varieties. They also employ advanced agronomic practices, such as precision farming, to optimize planting, irrigation, and pest management. By doing so, they help farmers produce more food with fewer resources, minimizing the environmental impact of agriculture.

In livestock management, agriculturists focus on animal breeding, nutrition, and health. They work to improve the productivity, welfare, and sustainability of various livestock species, such as cattle, pigs, poultry, and fish. Their efforts include developing efficient feeding strategies, monitoring animal health, and implementing disease prevention and control measures.

To become an agriculturist, one typically obtains a bachelor's degree in agriculture, agronomy, animal science, or a related field. Advanced positions may require a master's or doctoral degree, with specialized coursework in crop production, animal husbandry, or agricultural management.

A fascinating example of an agriculturist's impact can be found in the development of drought-tolerant crop varieties. By harnessing plant genetics and advanced breeding techniques, agriculturists have created crops that can thrive in water-scarce environments, helping to secure food production in the face of climate change.

In conclusion, agriculturists are dedicated professionals who apply their knowledge of plant and animal sciences, soil management, and modern farming techniques to optimize agricultural production. Their work is vital in addressing global challenges such as food security, climate change, and sustainable resource management.

AIR TRAFFIC CONTROLLER

An air traffic controller is a highly trained professional responsible for coordinating and guiding aircraft in the skies and on the ground. These individuals play a vital role in maintaining the safety, efficiency, and smooth operation of the aviation industry, ensuring that flights arrive and depart in a timely and orderly manner.

Air traffic controllers are skilled communicators who provide pilots with crucial information and instructions. They monitor aircraft positions, speed, and altitude using radar and other sophisticated technology, keeping a watchful eye on the airspace to prevent collisions and maintain optimal flight paths. Their expertise in navigation, weather, and aviation regulations is crucial in helping pilots make informed decisions during flight.

There are several specialized roles within the field of air traffic control. Tower controllers work in control towers at airports, where they oversee aircraft movements on runways and taxiways. They are responsible for coordinating takeoffs, landings, and ground traffic, ensuring that planes maintain safe distances from one another.

En-route controllers, on the other hand, work in Area Control Centers (ACCs), managing aircraft as they travel through high-altitude airspace. They provide pilots with altitude adjustments, route changes, and other instructions to maintain a safe and efficient flow of traffic. Terminal controllers guide planes as they approach or depart from busy airports, assisting with transitions between en-route and tower control zones.

The profession of air traffic control demands exceptional concentration, decision-making, and communication skills. Controllers must be able to perform under pressure, as they are responsible for the safety of thousands of passengers daily. They work in rotating shifts, often during weekends, holidays, and nights, to ensure round-the-clock coverage of airspace and airports.

To become an air traffic controller, candidates must typically complete a rigorous selection process and training program, which may include a combination of classroom instruction, simulation exercises, and on-the-job training. In many countries, such as the United States, prospective controllers must also pass a series of examinations and obtain certification from their national aviation authority.

ANESTHESIOLOGIST

An anesthesiologist is a medical doctor who specializes in the administration of anesthesia and the management of pain during and after surgical procedures, as well as in other medical contexts. These professionals play a critical role in ensuring patient safety, comfort, and optimal outcomes in various medical settings.

Before surgery, anesthesiologists review patients' medical histories, perform physical examinations, and evaluate factors such as age, weight, and pre-existing conditions to determine the most appropriate anesthesia plan. They discuss the options with patients and obtain informed consent, ensuring that individuals understand the risks and benefits of the chosen method.

During surgery, anesthesiologists administer anesthesia to keep patients pain-free and unconscious, or sedated, as needed. They monitor vital signs such as heart rate, blood pressure, and oxygen levels, adjusting the anesthesia and other medications as required to maintain the patient's stability. They also work closely with the surgical team, providing updates on the patient's condition and responding to any complications that may arise.

After surgery, anesthesiologists oversee patients' recovery from anesthesia, managing pain and addressing any side effects. They may also be involved in the treatment of acute and chronic pain in non-surgical settings, providing pain-relief interventions for conditions such as cancer, trauma, or chronic diseases.

Becoming an anesthesiologist requires extensive education and training. After completing a bachelor's degree, candidates must attend medical school and earn a Doctor of Medicine (MD) or Doctor of Osteopathic Medicine (DO) degree. Following medical school, they must complete a residency program in anesthesiology, which typically lasts four years. Some anesthesiologists choose to pursue additional fellowship training in a specialized area, such as cardiac anesthesia or pain medicine.

A compelling example of an anesthesiologist's impact can be found in the field of organ transplantation. Anesthesiologists play a critical role in ensuring the safety and comfort of both the organ donor and recipient during complex transplant procedures.

With numerous specializations and practice settings to choose from, a career in anesthesiology offers a challenging and rewarding path for those dedicated to improving patient outcomes and contributing to the advancement of medical care.

ANTHROPOLOGIST

An anthropologist is a social scientist who studies the origins, development, and behavior of human societies, both past and present. They explore diverse aspects of human experience, such as culture, language, biology, and social organization, to better understand our shared humanity and the complexities of the human experience across time and space. Anthropologists typically specialize in one of three main subfields: cultural, linguistic, and biological.

Cultural anthropologists focus on the beliefs, customs, and social institutions of contemporary societies. They conduct fieldwork by living with communities, observing their daily lives, and participating in their activities to gain a deep understanding of their cultural practices and values.

Linguistic anthropologists study the role of language in human societies, exploring the structure, evolution, and social functions of languages. They investigate how communication shapes social dynamics, identity, and cultural expression, and how it influences our understanding of the world.

Biological or physical anthropologists examine the biological aspects of humans and our closest relatives, such as primates. They study human evolution, genetics, and adaptations to various environments. This subfield also includes the study of primatology, forensic anthropology, and human osteology.

Anthropologists work in a range of settings, including universities, research institutions, museums, government agencies, and non-profit organizations. Some also work in the private sector, applying their expertise in cultural understanding to areas such as marketing, human resources, and international development.

An intriguing example of an anthropologist's impact can be seen in the field of cultural preservation. By documenting endangered languages, rituals, and traditions, anthropologists help to preserve the rich diversity of human cultures and foster greater appreciation and understanding among different societies.

In conclusion, anthropologists are dedicated social scientists who explore the multifaceted nature of human societies and cultures. Their work sheds light on our shared humanity and enhances our understanding of the diverse experiences that define us.

ARCHAEOLOGIST

An archaeologist is like a time traveler. They study artifacts and remains from the past to learn more about how people lived a long time ago.

Have you ever wondered what life was like hundreds or even thousands of years ago? Archaeologists are the people who try to answer that question. They study artifacts and remains left behind by people in the past to learn more about how they lived, what they ate, how they worked, and even what they believed.

Archaeologists study many different things from the past. They study buildings, such as houses, temples, and castles, to learn more about how people built and lived in them. They study tools and weapons to learn how people worked and defended themselves; pottery and other artifacts to learn about how people made and used them; and bones and other remains to learn more about what people ate and how they lived.

One of the most exciting things that archaeologists study are ancient civilizations. These are groups of people who lived a long time ago and built complex societies. Some of the most famous ancient civilizations are the Egyptians, the Greeks, the Romans, and the Maya. Archaeologists study the remains of these civilizations to learn more about their way of life, their art and architecture, and even their religion.

But being an archaeologist isn't just about digging in the dirt. They also use science to analyze the artifacts and remains they find. For example, they might use carbon dating to determine how old an object is, or use DNA analysis to learn more about the people who lived in the past. They also use technology like Lidar to create 3D models of buildings or other items, which can help them understand how they were used.

One of the most important things that archaeologists do is share their discoveries with others. They write scientific papers and give presentations at conferences to share what they've learned. They also work with local communities to ensure that the artifacts and remains are protected and preserved for future generations to study and learn from.

So, if you're curious about the past and like solving mysteries, archaeology might be the job for you. No matter if you work for a university, a research institute, or even a museum, there are many different opportunities for archaeologists. And who knows, maybe one day you'll be the one discovering a lost city or uncovering a hidden treasure!

ARCHITECT

An architect is someone who designs, plans, and oversees the construction of buildings and structures, shaping the built environment and contributing to the functionality and aesthetic appeal of cities, towns, and communities. Architects play a vital role in creating spaces that meet the needs of their inhabitants while also considering sustainability, cultural context, and the evolving nature of urban and rural landscapes.

Architects begin their design process by consulting with clients to understand their needs, preferences, and budget constraints. They conduct site analyses, consider environmental factors, and examine local building codes and regulations to ensure compliance. Through sketches, 3D models, and computer-aided design (CAD) tools, architects create detailed plans that incorporate structural, mechanical, electrical, and plumbing systems, as well as aesthetic elements such as materials, finishes, and landscaping.

Collaboration is an essential aspect of an architect's work. They engage with a wide range of professionals, including engineers, urban planners, landscape architects, interior designers, and construction managers, to develop comprehensive building designs that address the complex interplay of form, function, and context. Architects also oversee the construction process, working closely with contractors to ensure that projects are executed according to the design specifications, budget, and schedule.

To become an architect, one typically completes a professional degree in architecture, such as a Bachelor's or a Master's of Architecture. Following their education, aspiring architects and must pass a licensing examination, such as the Architect Registration Examination (ARE) in the United States, to become registered professionals.

Architects can specialize in various areas, such as residential, commercial, or institutional design, or focus on specific building types, such as healthcare facilities, educational institutions, or transportation hubs. They may also concentrate on particular aspects of the design process, such as sustainability, historic preservation, or urban design.

An inspiring example of an architect's impact can be seen in the development of eco-friendly, energy-efficient buildings. By incorporating innovative technologies, materials, and design strategies, architects create structures that minimize their environmental footprint, promote occupant well-being, and contribute to the long-term resilience of communities.

ART DIRECTOR

Art directors are creative professionals who design visual elements for a wide range of media, including advertising, television and film, publishing, and digital media. They are responsible for the overall look and feel of a project, and work closely with a team of designers, illustrators, photographers, and other artists to achieve the desired outcome.

One of the primary roles of an art director is to conceptualize and develop the creative direction for a project. This involves developing a visual language that will communicate the message or story in a way that is engaging and effective. Art directors typically work closely with clients or producers to understand the project goals, and then collaborate with their team to develop ideas and concepts.

Once the creative direction has been established, the art director is responsible for overseeing the development of all visual elements, including the selection of colors, typography, and imagery. They work with designers and other artists to create sketches and mockups, and provide feedback and guidance throughout the design process to ensure that the final product meets the project's goals.

Art directors are also responsible for managing the production of the project, including overseeing photo and video shoots, coordinating with printing and manufacturing vendors, and ensuring that all aspects of the design process are completed on time and within budget.

In addition to their creative work, art directors often have managerial responsibilities, including hiring and training new team members, setting budgets and timelines, and managing client relationships. They may also be responsible for marketing and promoting their team's work, and for developing and maintaining relationships with clients and vendors.

To be successful in this role, art directors must have a strong creative vision, as well as excellent leadership and communication skills. They must be able to work collaboratively with other artists and team members, while also being able to provide clear direction and guidance. They should be familiar with a wide range of design tools and technologies, and should be able to stay up-to-date with the latest trends and techniques in their field.

Art directors often have a degree in graphic design, fine arts, or a related field, and may have previous experience working as a designer or illustrator. They may work for advertising agencies, design firms, publishers, or other creative industries.

ASTRONAUT

Astronauts are among the most iconic and fascinating professionals on the planet. They are a select group of people who have been chosen to explore the final frontier: space. With a passion for science, engineering, and exploration, these brave men and women venture into the unknown, facing challenges that are unlike anything faced by most other professions.

At its core, the role of an astronaut is to explore space. This involves piloting spacecraft, performing scientific experiments, and conducting research on behalf of space agencies such as NASA, the European Space Agency (ESA), and the Russian Space Agency (Roscosmos). To be considered for the role of an astronaut, individuals must undergo rigorous training and meet certain physical and intellectual requirements.

The journey to become an astronaut typically begins with a background in science or engineering, as well as experience as a pilot or military aviator. Prospective astronauts must also meet certain physical requirements, such as being in excellent physical shape and having excellent vision. Additionally, astronauts must have strong communication skills and the ability to work well in a team environment.

Once selected, astronauts are trained in a variety of skills that are essential for space travel. This includes learning how to pilot spacecraft, performing spacewalks, and conducting scientific experiments in microgravity. Astronauts are also trained to respond to emergencies that may arise during their missions, such as fires or equipment failures.

The role of an astronaut is constantly evolving, as new technologies and discoveries are made in the field of space exploration. Today, astronauts are involved in a wide range of activities, from exploring other planets to working on the International Space Station (ISS). They work closely with engineers and scientists on the ground to conduct experiments that help us better understand the universe and our place in it.

One of the most challenging aspects of being an astronaut is the physical toll that space travel can take on the body. In space, there is no gravity, which means that the body is exposed to a number of new and unique physical stresses. These include loss of bone density, muscle atrophy, and changes in vision. To combat these effects, astronauts must undergo a rigorous exercise regimen and be closely monitored by medical professionals.

Despite the many challenges that come with being an astronaut, there are few professions that offer the same level of excitement and adventure. With the ongoing exploration of space and the possibility of future missions to other planets, the role of the astronaut is more important than ever.

ASTRONOMER

An astronomer is like a space detective. They study the stars, planets, and other objects in the sky to learn more about our universe.

Have you ever looked up at the night sky and wondered what's up there? Astronomers are the people who try to answer that question. They use telescopes and other special equipment to observe and study the objects in the sky. They also use math and science to analyze the data they collect.

Astronomers study many different things in the sky. They study stars, which are big balls of hot gas that light up the sky at night. They also study planets, which are like Earth but might have different atmospheres, surfaces, and even life. Astronomers study galaxies, which are groups of stars and other objects that are held together by gravity. They also study black holes, which are places where gravity is so strong that nothing can escape, not even light!

One of the most exciting things that astronomers study are exoplanets. These are planets that orbit stars other than our sun. Astronomers use special techniques to detect these planets, which can be very hard to see because they are so far away. By studying these planets, astronomers hope to learn more about the possibility of life beyond planet Earth.

But being an astronomer isn't just about looking through a telescope. They also use computer programs to analyze the data they collect. For example, they might use math to figure out how far away a star is or how fast a planet is moving. They also use computer simulations to help them understand complex processes, such as how stars are born.

One of the most important things that astronomers do is share their discoveries with others. They write scientific papers and give presentations at conferences to share what they've learned. They also work together with other scientists from around the world to collaborate and share information. By doing this, they can learn even more about our universe.

So, if you're curious about the universe and like solving mysteries, astronomy might be the job for you. Whether you work for a university, a research institute, or even NASA, there are many different opportunities for astronomers. And who knows, maybe one day you'll be the one discovering new planets or studying the mysteries of the universe!

AUDIOLOGIST

An audiologist is a healthcare professional who specializes in the diagnosis, treatment, and management of hearing and balance disorders. Their work is essential in helping people of all ages, from infants to the elderly, overcome hearing impairments and maintain good auditory health, ultimately enhancing their overall quality of life.

Audiologists assess hearing and balance function through comprehensive evaluations, using advanced testing techniques and equipment to identify the type, degree, and cause of hearing loss or balance disorders. They interpret test results and develop personalized treatment plans to address the specific needs of each patient.

One of the primary interventions provided by audiologists is the selection, fitting, and adjustment of hearing aids or other assistive listening devices. They ensure that devices are tailored to the patient's specific hearing requirements and provide education on proper usage, care, and maintenance. Audiologists also offer guidance on strategies to improve communication and cope with hearing loss, such as lip-reading, sign language, or auditory training.

In cases where hearing aids are not sufficient, audiologists may recommend cochlear implants or other medical interventions. They collaborate with otolaryngologists, speech-language pathologists, and other healthcare professionals to provide comprehensive care for patients with more complex hearing and balance disorders.

To become an audiologist, one typically completes a Doctor of Audiology degree, which involves coursework in areas such as acoustics, anatomy, physiology, audiology diagnostics, and hearing aid technology.

A captivating example of an audiologist's impact can be found in the early identification and intervention of hearing loss in newborns. By conducting newborn hearing screenings, audiologists can detect hearing impairments at a critical stage, enabling prompt treatment and support to optimize language development and social functioning.

In conclusion, audiologists are dedicated healthcare professionals who diagnose and treat hearing and balance disorders, playing a crucial role in enhancing the auditory health and well-being of individuals across the lifespan. Their expertise in assessment, intervention, and patient education is essential in helping people overcome hearing impairments and lead fulfilling lives.

AUDITOR

Auditors are professionals who ensure the accuracy of a company or organization's financial records. They examine records to make sure that transactions are recorded correctly, money is being spent appropriately, and financial statements are accurate. The auditor's job is to make sure that the company is following all the rules and regulations set by the government, and that the public can trust the financial statements of the company.

Imagine you're a manager of a company. You have a lot of responsibilities, but one of the most important is making sure that the company's finances are in order. It's not just about making a profit, but also making sure that you're following the law and reporting everything correctly. This is where an auditor comes in.

Auditors use a variety of techniques to check the financial records. They look at bank statements, invoices, receipts, and other documents to make sure that everything is accounted for. They also talk to employees and management to understand how money is being spent and to verify that the financial records are accurate.

The auditor's job is to identify any mistakes or fraud that may be happening. They check for any suspicious transactions or unexplained discrepancies in the records. If something looks suspicious, they will investigate further to find out what's going on.

The auditor's role is very important in maintaining the trust of investors and the public. If a company's financial statements are found to be inaccurate, it can have serious consequences. Investors may lose money, and the company's reputation may be damaged. The auditor helps prevent this by making sure that the financial statements are accurate and that the company is following all the rules.

One of the challenges of being an auditor is maintaining independence and objectivity. Auditors need to be impartial and not influenced by any personal or financial interests. This ensures that they can provide an unbiased opinion on the financial statements. Another challenge is keeping up with changing laws and regulations. Auditors need to stay up to date with the latest changes in accounting standards and regulations to make sure that they are providing accurate information.

AVIATION TECHNICIAN

Aviation technicians, also known as aircraft mechanics or aircraft maintenance technicians, are responsible for ensuring that aircraft are safe to fly. They work on airplanes, helicopters, and other types of aircraft, performing routine maintenance, repairs, and inspections. Aviation technicians play a critical role in the aviation industry, as they are responsible for the safety of passengers and crew.

Aviation technicians are highly skilled professionals who work in a variety of different environments, including airports, maintenance hangars, and repair shops. They may work on large commercial airliners or small private planes, and they must be familiar with a wide range of aircraft systems, including engines, electrical systems, avionics, and flight controls. Their work can involve anything from changing oil and filters to repairing hydraulic systems and engines.

One of the most important aspects of an aviation technician's job is performing routine maintenance on aircraft. This can involve inspecting the aircraft, checking fluid levels, and replacing worn or damaged parts. Technicians may also be responsible for making repairs, such as fixing leaks or replacing broken parts. They use a variety of tools and equipment, including hand and power tools, gauges, and diagnostic equipment, to diagnose and fix problems.

In addition to performing routine maintenance, aviation technicians are responsible for conducting inspections of aircraft to ensure they are airworthy. This involves checking every aspect of the aircraft, from the landing gear and brakes to the engines and cockpit controls. If any problems are found during an inspection, the technician must make the necessary repairs before the aircraft is cleared to fly.

Aviation technicians must also be able to read and interpret technical manuals and schematics, as well as keep up-to-date with the latest technologies and regulations in the industry. They must be able to work quickly and accurately under pressure, as aircraft downtime can be costly for airlines and other aviation companies. In addition, they must be able to communicate effectively with other members of the maintenance team and with pilots and other aviation professionals.

Aviation technicians typically work in shifts, as aircraft need to be serviced around the clock. They may work evenings, weekends, and holidays, and they must be able to work in all types of weather conditions. The job can be physically demanding, as technicians may need to climb ladders, work in tight spaces, and lift heavy equipment.

BACK-END DEVELOPER

A back-end developer is a type of software developer who is responsible for building the server-side of web applications. This means that they are focused on making sure that the server, database, and other components of an application are all functioning properly and communicating with each other seamlessly.

While front-end developers are more focused on the visual aspects of a web application, such as the layout and design, back-end developers are more focused on the functionality of the application. They work on the parts of the application that are not seen by the user, such as the application's architecture, data storage, and security.

To accomplish these tasks, back-end developers use a variety of programming languages, such as Python, Ruby, and Java. They work with different databases, like MySQL, MongoDB, and PostgreSQL, to store and retrieve data. Additionally, they use various tools and frameworks, such as Node.js, Express, and Django, to create server-side applications.

One of the most important aspects of being a back-end developer is understanding how to write code that is both efficient and secure. Back-end developers must ensure that their code can handle large amounts of traffic and data, and that it is not vulnerable to attacks by malicious hackers.

Back-end developers often work closely with front-end developers, as well as project managers and designers, to ensure that an application is functioning as intended. They collaborate to ensure that the user experience is seamless and that the application is meeting the needs of the client or organization.

Another important aspect of being a back-end developer is the ability to troubleshoot and debug issues that arise within the application. This can involve identifying and fixing bugs, optimizing code for better performance, and making changes to the application's architecture to ensure scalability.

Besides technical skills, back-end developers also need to have strong problem-solving, analytical, and communication skills. They need to be able to work effectively as part of a team, as well as be able to work independently to solve complex technical problems.

In conclusion, back-end development is a crucial component of modern web development. It is a challenging and dynamic career path that requires a combination of technical and soft skills. Back-end developers are essential in creating high-performing, secure, and scalable web applications that are used by millions of people every day.

BAKER

A baker is someone who makes delicious baked goods like bread, cakes, cookies, and pastries. They use their creativity and knowledge of ingredients to create tasty treats that people can enjoy any time of day.

Baking is an art as well as a science, and bakers need to be precise in measuring and mixing ingredients to create the perfect texture and flavor in their baked goods. They also need to know how to work with different types of flour, sugar, and yeast to create different types of bread and other baked goods.

One of the best things about being a baker is that you get to experiment with different flavors and ingredients to create unique and tasty treats. You can mix in fruits, nuts, and spices to create something new and exciting. And when you get the perfect balance of flavors and textures, there's nothing quite as satisfying as seeing someone take a bite of your creation and smile with joy.

Bakers often work in bakeries, which can be big and commercial or small and family-owned. They might work alone or as part of a team, depending on the size of the bakery. Bakers might work very early in the morning to get the bread ready for the day, or work late into the night to get everything prepared for the next day.

Bakers also need to have a good understanding of food safety and sanitation practices, to make sure their baked goods are safe and healthy to eat. They need to keep their work areas clean and organized, and follow strict guidelines for storing and handling food.

If you're interested in becoming a baker, there are a few things you should know. First, you'll need to have a love for baking and enjoy working with your hands. You'll also need to be patient, since some baked goods can take a long time to prepare and cook.

In addition, you'll need to have a good understanding of math, since baking involves a lot of measuring and precise calculations. You'll also need to be able to work under pressure, since baking can be a fast-paced and stressful environment at times.

Baking can be a really fun and fulfilling career. There's nothing quite like the smell of fresh-baked bread or the taste of a warm chocolate chip cookie straight out of the oven. If you're passionate about baking and enjoy creating delicious treats, it might be the perfect job for you.

BARBER

A barber is a skilled professional who cuts and styles hair. They work in barbershops, which are often small and cozy places where people come to get a haircut or a shave. Barbers have been around for centuries, and they play an important role in society by helping people look and feel their best.

One of the perks of being a barber is that you get to use your creativity and skills to help people look their best. You get to work with different types of hair and facial hair, and you get to create different styles to suit your clients' preferences. Whether someone wants a classic look or something trendy and modern, you get to use your skills and experience to make it happen.

Barbers use a variety of tools to cut and style hair, including scissors, clippers, and combs. They need to be skilled in using these tools to create different types of cuts and styles, and they need to be able to work quickly and efficiently to keep up with the demands of their clients.

Besides cutting hair, barbers also provide other services like shaves and beard trims. They need to be skilled in using a razor and other tools to create a clean and precise shave, and they need to be able to work with different types of skin to avoid irritation or razor burn.

In addition to their technical skills, barbers must possess strong interpersonal and communication abilities, as they often engage in conversation with clients during appointments. This rapport helps create a welcoming and enjoyable atmosphere in the barbershop, fostering long-term customer relationships and repeat business.

To become a barber, one typically attends a barbering or cosmetology school, where they learn the foundational skills and techniques required for the profession, such as haircutting, shaving, and sanitation practices. After completing their education, aspiring barbers must obtain a license to practice in their jurisdiction, which usually involves passing a written exam and a practical skills assessment.

Being a barber can be a gratifying career. You get to use your creativity and skills to help people look and feel their best, and you get to work in a cozy and welcoming environment. If you enjoy cutting hair and helping people look their best, it might be the perfect job for you.

BARISTA

A barista is a skilled and experienced professional who prepares and serves coffee-based drinks. As coffee culture has grown in popularity over the years, so has the importance of the barista in the coffee shop industry.

At its most basic level, a barista is responsible for making a variety of coffee drinks, including espresso, cappuccino, latte, and Americano. They are also responsible for taking customer orders, handling cash and other forms of payment, and ensuring that the coffee shop runs smoothly.

However, the role of the barista is much more complex than simply making coffee. A barista must have a deep understanding of coffee beans, brewing techniques, and flavor profiles. They need to be able to adjust their techniques to suit different types of beans and roasts, and be able to make adjustments to the grind and water temperature to ensure that each cup of coffee is perfect.

Baristas must also have excellent customer service skills. They are the face of the coffee shop, and they must be able to interact with customers in a friendly and professional manner. They must be able to answer questions about the different types of coffee and make recommendations based on the customer's taste preferences.

In addition to their coffee making skills, baristas are often responsible for maintaining and cleaning the equipment used in the coffee shop, including the espresso machine and the grinder. They must ensure that these machines are in good working order and that they are cleaned and maintained regularly to ensure that they continue to produce high-quality coffee drinks.

Another important aspect of a barista's job is creating latte art. This involves using steamed milk to create intricate designs on the surface of a latte or cappuccino. Latte art has become an important part of the coffee shop experience, and a skilled barista can create beautiful and intricate designs that are as much a work of art as they are a delicious beverage.

Overall, the role of the barista is one that requires a combination of technical skill, creativity, and excellent customer service. A great barista has a deep understanding of coffee and brewing techniques, can create delicious and visually appealing coffee drinks, and is able to interact with customers in a friendly and professional manner. Whether you are in need of a morning pick-me-up or a place to relax with friends, the barista plays a critical role in creating a welcoming and enjoyable coffee shop experience.

BARTENDER

A bartender is a skilled professional who works in a bar or pub, serving drinks and sometimes food to customers. They play an important role in creating a fun and enjoyable atmosphere for people to relax and socialize in.

One of the most exciting parts of being a bartender is that you get to meet lots of interesting people from all walks of life. You get to talk to people from all around the world, and you get to learn about their lives and experiences. You also get to help create a fun and social atmosphere for people to enjoy, whether they're celebrating a special occasion or just having a casual drink with friends.

Bartenders are responsible for creating and serving drinks to their customers. They need to be knowledgeable about different types of alcohol and mixers, as well as how to create a variety of cocktails and other drinks. They also need to be skilled in using the equipment and tools that are used to create and serve drinks, such as shakers, strainers, and glasses.

In addition to creating and serving drinks, bartenders are also responsible for keeping the bar clean and well-stocked. They need to be able to work quickly and efficiently to make sure that their customers are always happy and satisfied. They also need to be able to multitask, since they might need to take orders from several customers at once and keep track of multiple drink orders.

Bartenders also play an important role in ensuring that their customers are safe and responsible. They need to be able to recognize when someone has had too much to drink, and they need to know when it's time to cut someone off or call a taxi for them. They also need to be knowledgeable about the laws and regulations related to serving alcohol, such as checking IDs and not serving alcohol to minors.

In addition, you'll need to be able to work well under pressure, since bartending can be a fast-paced and busy job in sometimes a noisy environment. You'll also need to be able to work flexible hours, since many bars and pubs are open late into the night.

Being a bartender can be a really fun and exciting career. You get to meet lots of interesting people, create and serve delicious drinks, and help people have a great time. If you're passionate about socializing, mixology, and creating a fun atmosphere for people to enjoy, go for it!

BIOCHEMIST

Biochemists are scientists who study the chemical processes and substances that occur in living organisms, from the tiniest cells to the largest animals. Biochemists use their knowledge to help us better understand how living organisms work and how we can develop new treatments for diseases.

Biochemists explore the structure, function, and interactions of biomolecules, such as proteins, nucleic acids, lipids, and carbohydrates. They investigate how these molecules contribute to essential biological processes like metabolism, cell signaling, gene expression, and cellular development. Through their research, biochemists aim to uncover the molecular basis of health and disease, opening up new avenues for prevention, diagnosis, and treatment.

One of the primary techniques used by biochemists is the isolation and analysis of biomolecules. They employ a variety of laboratory methods, such as chromatography, electrophoresis, and mass spectrometry, to separate, identify, and quantify the components of complex biological samples. Additionally, biochemists use advanced imaging techniques, like X-ray crystallography and cryo-electron microscopy, to visualize molecular structures and gain insights into their function.

To become a biochemist, one typically earns a bachelor's degree in biochemistry, chemistry, or a related field, followed by a master's or doctoral degree in biochemistry or a specialized area of study. This advanced education involves coursework in subjects like organic chemistry, physical chemistry, molecular biology, and genetics, as well as hands-on laboratory research.

Biochemists work in diverse settings, including academic institutions, research institutes, pharmaceutical companies, biotechnology firms, and government agencies. Their research spans a wide range of applications, from developing new drugs and therapies to enhancing crop yields and addressing environmental challenges.

An inspiring example of a biochemist's impact can be seen in the development of life-saving medications, such as targeted cancer therapies. By elucidating the molecular pathways that drive cancer cell growth, biochemists have contributed to the creation of drugs that specifically target these pathways, offering more effective and less toxic treatments for cancer patients.

BIOMEDICAL ENGINEER

Biomedical engineers are scientists and engineers who use their knowledge of biology, medicine, and engineering to create new medical technologies and devices that help people live healthier and happier lives. Biomedical engineers are important members of the healthcare team, working alongside doctors, nurses, and other medical professionals to create and improve medical devices, from artificial limbs to heart pumps.

As a biomedical engineer, you can work on designing and developing medical devices such as pacemakers, artificial limbs, and imaging machines that allow doctors to see inside the human body.

One of the coolest things about being a biomedical engineer is that you get to use your creativity to solve real-world problems that can have a huge impact on people's lives. For example, you might work on creating a device that can help people with Parkinson's disease control their tremors, or you might work on developing a new drug that can slow the progression of Alzheimer's.

Biomedical engineers also use a lot of advanced technology in their work, including 3D printers that can create custom prosthetics and implants, and computer models that can simulate the effects of drugs and medical treatments on the body.

In addition to developing new technologies, biomedical engineers also are in charge of testing and evaluating medical devices to make sure they are safe and effective. This can involve conducting clinical trials on human subjects to determine the efficacy of a new treatment or device, or working with regulatory agencies to ensure that medical devices meet safety and quality standards.

If you're interested in becoming a biomedical engineer, here is a path you could take. First, you'll need to have a strong background in science and math, including courses in biology, chemistry, physics, and calculus. You'll also need to complete a bachelor's degree in biomedical engineering or a related field, and many biomedical engineers also go on to earn a master's or a PhD.

Once you've completed your education, you can find a job in a variety of settings, including hospitals, research labs, medical device companies, and government agencies. No matter where you work, you'll have the opportunity to make a real difference in people's lives by developing new technologies and treatments.

BLOCKCHAIN ENGINEER

A blockchain engineer is a specialized software developer who focuses on creating, implementing, and maintaining blockchain technology solutions. Their work is crucial in advancing the applications of blockchain, a decentralized digital ledger system, in industries such as finance, supply chain management, and data security.

Blockchain engineers design and develop the architecture of blockchain systems, which involves creating consensus algorithms, data structures, and cryptographic protocols. They ensure that blockchain networks are secure, scalable, and efficient, enabling users to conduct transactions and exchange information without relying on centralized authorities.

These professionals also build and maintain smart contracts, which are self-executing agreements with the terms directly written into code. Smart contracts automate transactions and enforce contract conditions, providing increased transparency, efficiency, and trust in various applications, such as decentralized finance (DeFi) platforms and tokenized asset management.

To integrate blockchain technology with existing systems, blockchain engineers develop and maintain Application Programming Interfaces (APIs), which enable communication between blockchain networks and external applications. They also ensure that the performance, security, and compliance requirements of these integrations are met, addressing potential issues and vulnerabilities.

To become a blockchain engineer, one typically earns a bachelor's degree in computer science, software engineering, or a related field, or acquires equivalent skills through self-directed learning or coding boot camps. Proficiency in programming languages, such as JavaScript, Python, or Solidity, is essential, as is experience with blockchain platforms like Ethereum, Hyperledger, or Binance Smart Chain. Familiarity with cryptographic principles, distributed systems, and networking protocols is also crucial for success.

Blockchain engineers work in a variety of industries, such as finance, healthcare, logistics, and technology. They may be employed by start-ups, established corporations, or as freelancers, consultants, or remote workers.

As the field of blockchain technology continues to grow, blockchain engineers are in high demand. Many large companies and startups are investing heavily in blockchain technology, and the need for skilled professionals is only increasing. This means that blockchain engineers have excellent job prospects and may be able to command high salaries.

BOOK AGENT

A book agent, also known as a literary agent, is a professional who represents and advocates for authors in the book publishing industry. A book agent's primary role is to help authors get their work published by connecting them with publishing houses and negotiating book deals on their behalf. While book agents are most commonly associated with the publishing of novels, they can also represent a variety of non-fiction genres, such as memoirs, cookbooks, and self-help books.

One of the primary responsibilities of a book agent is to act as a mediator between an author and a publisher. They work closely with authors to help them perfect their manuscripts and prepare book proposals that will be attractive to publishers. Once an agent has identified a suitable publisher for a client, they will then pitch the book to that publisher and negotiate the terms of the deal, including the author's advance and royalties.

Beyond securing book deals for their clients, book agents also provide a range of other services to help authors succeed in the publishing industry. For example, they may help authors navigate the editorial process, provide marketing and publicity support, and offer guidance on building a long-term writing career.

To become a book agent, one typically needs a combination of strong writing skills, an understanding of the publishing industry, and excellent communication and negotiation skills. Many book agents begin their careers in publishing by working as an editor or working in a literary agency in a junior position before moving up the ranks. Others may have experience as a writer, journalist, or in a related field.

Book agents play an important role in the publishing industry, as they help ensure that the best writing gets published and that authors receive fair compensation for their work. They act as the primary liaison between authors and publishers and help authors navigate the complex world of publishing. Without book agents, many great books may never see the light of day, and many talented authors may never get the recognition they deserve.

Overall, book agents are passionate advocates for literature and play a vital role in the creative process of bringing new books to the world. They help to identify and develop the best writing talent, guide authors through the often-daunting publishing process, and support authors in building long-term writing careers. If you are an aspiring author looking to break into the publishing industry, working with a book agent can be a crucial step in achieving your dreams.

BREWER

A brewer is someone who makes delicious beverages like beer and cider. They use their creativity and knowledge of ingredients to create unique and flavorful drinks that people can enjoy with friends and family.

Brewing is a mixture of art and science, and brewers need to be precise in measuring and mixing ingredients to create the perfect balance of flavors and aromas in their beverages. They also need to know how to work with different types of grains, hops, and yeast to create different styles of beer or cider.

One of the best things about being a brewer is that you get to experiment with different flavors and ingredients to create new and exciting beverages. You can mix in fruits, spices, and herbs to create something unique and delicious. And when you get the perfect balance of flavors and aromas, there's nothing quite as satisfying as seeing someone take a sip of your creation and smile with joy.

Brewers work in breweries, which can be big and commercial or small and independent. They might work alone or as part of a team, depending on the size of the brewery. Brewers might work very early in the morning to get the mash ready for the day or work late into the night to monitor the fermentation process.

Brewers also need to have a good understanding of the science behind brewing, including the chemistry of fermentation. They need to know how to control the temperature, pH, and oxygen levels during the brewing process to ensure a consistent high-quality product.

If you're interested in becoming a brewer, there are a few things you should know. First, you'll need to have a passion for brewing and enjoy working with your hands. You'll also need to be patient, since brewing can take a long time and requires attention to detail.

In addition, you'll need to have a good understanding of math, because brewing involves a lot of measuring and precise calculations. You'll also need to be able to work well under pressure as brewing can be a fast-paced and demanding environment at times.

Brewing can be a really fun and rewarding career. For some people there's nothing quite like the taste of a fresh, cold beer on a hot summer day, or the warmth of a spicy cider on a chilly winter night. If you're passionate about brewing and enjoy creating delicious beverages, it might be the perfect job for you.

BUSINESS CONSULTANT

Business consultants are people who help companies solve problems and improve their performance. As a business consultant, you might work with a wide variety of companies, from small startups to large corporations, and help them with everything from marketing and sales to operations and finance.

One of the coolest things about being a business consultant is that you get to work with all kinds of people, from CEOs and executives to employees at all levels of the company. You'll use your expertise and knowledge to help these people solve complex problems and make better decisions that will help their company succeed.

So, what exactly does a business consultant do? Well, it really depends on the specific company and the problems they're facing. Some business consultants specialize in a particular area, such as marketing or operations, while others have a more general background and can help with a wide range of issues.

One common task for a business consultant is to analyze a company's performance and identify areas where they can improve. This might involve looking at financial statements, sales data, customer feedback, and other information to identify patterns and trends. Based on this analysis, the consultant will then make recommendations for how the company can improve, whether it's by streamlining their operations, developing new marketing strategies, or implementing better accounting practices.

Another important role for a business consultant is to help companies implement changes and new strategies. This might involve working with employees at all levels of the company to ensure that everyone understands the new goals and is on board with the changes.

As a business consultant, you'll also need to have strong communication skills. You'll need to be able to explain complex ideas and concepts in a clear and concise manner, and you'll need to be able to build trust and rapport with your clients so that they feel comfortable working with you.

To become a business consultant, you need to have a background in business, finance, or a related field. Many consultants also have advanced degrees, such as an MBA or a PhD. It's also important to have experience working in a corporate or business setting, so that you have a good understanding of the challenges and issues that companies face.

CAR MECHANIC

Car mechanics, also known as automotive technicians, are highly skilled professionals who diagnose, repair, and maintain cars, trucks, and other vehicles. They work in a wide range of settings, including auto repair shops, car dealerships, and even in their own garages. Car mechanics are essential to keeping our vehicles running safely and efficiently, and they ensure that our transportation infrastructure remains operational.

The work of a car mechanic can be incredibly varied, and no two days are ever the same. They may spend one day working on a complex engine repair, and the next day changing a set of brake pads. Some of the typical tasks that a car mechanic may undertake include:

- Conducting diagnostics tests to identify issues with the vehicle

- Repairing or replacing faulty parts, such as brakes, engines, and transmissions

- Conducting routine maintenance on vehicles, such as oil changes, tire rotations, and battery replacements

- Advising customers on the best course of action to take to keep their vehicles running smoothly

- Communicating with other professionals, such as parts suppliers and other mechanics, to get the job done

Car mechanics must have certain technical skills and knowledge, including a deep understanding of automotive engineering, electrical systems, and computer diagnostics. They must also be able to use a range of specialized tools and equipment, including hydraulic lifts, air compressors, and diagnostic scanners. Given the complexity of modern vehicles, car mechanics must be constantly learning and updating their skills to keep up with the latest advancements in automotive technology.

Perhaps one of the most interesting aspects of being a car mechanic is the opportunity to work on all sort of vehicles. From classic cars to the latest high-performance sports cars, a car mechanic will have the opportunity to work on a huge range of vehicles, each with its own unique set of challenges. This variety can help keep the job exciting.

Another interesting aspect of the job is the opportunity to work with a wide variety of customers. Car mechanics may interact with people from all kind, from wealthy car enthusiasts to budget-conscious drivers trying to keep an older vehicle running. This requires strong communication and interpersonal skills, as well as the ability to work efficiently and effectively under pressure.

CARDIOLOGIST

A cardiologist is a medical doctor who specializes in diagnosing and treating diseases and conditions related to the heart and blood vessels. They are trained to identify and treat conditions that affect the cardiovascular system, which includes the heart, blood vessels, and blood.

Cardiologists are experts in understanding the complex functions of the heart and circulatory system, and they are responsible for preventing, diagnosing, and treating a wide range of conditions that affect these vital organs. These conditions can include heart disease, heart attacks, heart rhythm disorders, and conditions related to blood vessels such as atherosclerosis, hypertension, and peripheral vascular disease.

Cardiologists use a wide range of tools and techniques to evaluate and diagnose heart and blood vessel problems, including physical examinations, medical imaging, and laboratory tests. They also use noninvasive tests such as electrocardiograms (EKGs), echocardiograms, and stress tests to evaluate the heart's function and detect any abnormalities. For more complicated cases, they may use more invasive procedures such as cardiac catheterization and angiography.

One of the primary roles of a cardiologist is to manage and treat heart disease, which is the leading cause of death in many countries around the world. They work with patients to develop personalized treatment plans that may include lifestyle changes, medications, and surgical procedures.

Cardiologists may also work in collaboration with other medical professionals, including primary care physicians, surgeons, and other specialists to ensure that patients receive comprehensive and coordinated care. They are often called upon to consult on complex cases and to provide second opinions, as well as to work with patients who have complex health issues that require specialized care.

Cardiologists also play a critical role in preventing heart disease and related conditions. They work to educate the public about heart health, risk factors, and strategies for prevention. They also work with other medical professionals to develop new and innovative treatments and technologies to improve outcomes for patients with heart and vascular disease.

In summary, a cardiologist is a highly trained medical professional who plays a vital role in the prevention, diagnosis, and treatment of heart disease and related conditions. They use their expertise to improve the health and well-being of their patients, as well as to advance the field of cardiovascular medicine through research and innovation.

CAREER COUNSELOR

A career counselor is a professional who helps individuals navigate the world of work and find fulfilling careers that match their interests, values, and skills. They use a variety of tools and techniques to help their clients explore different career paths, identify their strengths and weaknesses, and develop plans to achieve their career goals.

Career counselors work with people at various stages of their careers, from high school students exploring college majors to mid-career professionals looking to make a change. They help clients assess their interests, skills, and values through aptitude and personality tests, self-assessments, and other tools. They also help clients identify potential career paths that align with their strengths and interests, and provide guidance on how to achieve those goals.

In addition to helping clients identify and pursue career paths, career counselors also provide guidance on job search strategies, resume and cover letter writing, networking, and interview skills. They help clients navigate the job market by identifying job openings, preparing for job interviews, and negotiating job offers.

Career counselors also play a role in helping clients overcome obstacles that may be holding them back in their careers. They provide support and guidance to individuals struggling with job loss, career transitions, and other challenges. They may also help clients develop strategies to overcome obstacles related to issues such as disability, gender, race, or ethnicity.

Career counselors may work in a variety of settings, including colleges and universities, private career counseling firms, government agencies, and non-profit organizations. They may work with individuals in one-on-one sessions, or they may conduct group workshops or seminars on career development topics.

To be successful as a career counselor, one must have excellent communication and interpersonal skills, as well as a deep understanding of the job market and current trends in various industries. They must also have a strong knowledge of different career paths and how to match them with the needs and interests of their clients.

Overall, a career counselor is a valuable resource for anyone looking to find their path in the world of work. They provide guidance, support, and encouragement to help individuals achieve their career goals and find meaningful work that brings them satisfaction and fulfillment.

CARPENTER

Have you ever wanted to build a fort, a treehouse, or a cool bookshelf? If you have, then you might be interested in becoming a carpenter when you grow up!

Carpenters are skilled professionals who work with wood and other materials to build all sorts of things. They can work on large construction sites building houses and buildings, or they can work in small shops crafting custom-made furniture and other items. Carpenters are very important because they make it possible for people to have comfortable homes and beautiful buildings to work in.

One of the first things a carpenter does is read and interpret blueprints and plans for the project they will be working on. They use these plans to figure out how much wood and other materials they will need to complete the job. They also need to be very good at math because they have to measure everything very precisely to make sure it will all fit together correctly.

Once they have all the materials they need, carpenters use a variety of tools to cut, shape, and join the pieces of wood together. Some of the tools they use include saws, drills, hammers, and chisels. They also use special machines to shape the wood into curves and other interesting shapes. It's important for carpenters to be very careful when they're using these tools because they can be very sharp and dangerous if used incorrectly.

One of the coolest things about being a carpenter is that you get to see your work come to life right before your eyes. You start with a pile of wood and a set of plans, and by the time you're finished, you've created something beautiful and functional. Carpenters take a lot of pride in their work, and they should, because what they do is truly amazing!

Carpenters also have to be very physically fit because their work can be very strenuous. They have to be able to lift heavy pieces of wood, equipment, and work on their feet for long periods of time. They also have to be able to climb ladders and work on scaffolding to reach high places.

If you like working with your hands and creating things out of wood, then becoming a carpenter is the perfect career for you. It's a challenging but rewarding job that allows you to use your creativity and problem-solving skills to make the world a better place. Who knows, one day you might be building the house of your dreams or crafting a custom-made piece of furniture that will become famous.

CARTOGRAPHER

Have you ever looked at a map and wondered how it was made? Cartographers are the people who create maps! They take information from many sources and use it to create accurate and detailed maps of the world around us.

Cartographers use a combination of science, art, and technology to make maps. They work with a lot of different information, such as satellite imagery, aerial photography, and ground surveys. This information is then used to create maps that show things like land features, bodies of water, and even the locations of different buildings in a city.

To create these maps, cartographers use a variety of tools and software. One of the most important tools they use is called a geographic information system (GIS). This is a software program that helps cartographers organize and analyze data about the earth's surface. They also use specialized computer programs to create and edit maps, and they may use traditional art supplies like pencils and paper to create the initial drafts.

There are many different types of maps that cartographers create. Some maps are used for navigation, like road maps that show the best routes to take to get from one place to another. Other maps are used to study the environment, like topographical maps that show the elevation of different parts of the earth's surface. Still other maps are used to study demographics, such as population density or income distribution.

One of the most important skills for a cartographer is the ability to pay close attention to detail. They need to make sure that their maps are accurate and that they include all the information that someone might need. In addition to creating maps, need to keep up with new technology and methods for collecting and analyzing data. They also need to be aware of changes in the earth's surface, like new construction or natural disasters, and update their maps accordingly.

Cartographers work in many different settings. Some work for government agencies, creating maps for things like urban planning or emergency response. Others work for private companies, creating maps for things like marketing or real estate.

Overall, cartography is an important and interesting field that combines science, art, and technology. If you're interested in geography, technology, and art, you might enjoy becoming a cartographer!

CHEF

A chef is a culinary artist who transforms raw ingredients into delectable works of art, tantalizing the senses and igniting the passions of food lovers. From the humblest street food vendor to the most esteemed Michelin-starred maestro, chefs are the architects of flavor, texture, and aroma, who bring joy to the world through their craft.

A chef's journey begins with a deep reverence for ingredients, an insatiable curiosity for flavors, and a boundless imagination for culinary possibilities. They draw upon a vast array of techniques, traditions, and cultural influences, blending them into unique and harmonious culinary creations that delight the palate and warm the soul. A chef's tool kit includes an encyclopedic knowledge of ingredients, cooking methods, and food safety, as well as an unrelenting passion for experimentation and innovation.

Chefs work in a dizzying array of environments, from bustling restaurant kitchens to tranquil culinary schools, luxurious cruise ships, and high-stakes cooking competitions. They may specialize in a particular cuisine, such as French, Italian, or Japanese, or focus on a specific type of cooking, such as baking, grilling, or pastry. Many chefs have worked their way up through the ranks, starting as lowly line cooks and gradually ascending to the pinnacle of their profession through hard work, and perseverance.

To succeed as a chef, one must possess a complex set of skills and qualities, such as creativity, attention to detail, time management, leadership, and a love for teamwork. They must also be able to handle the heat and pressure of a busy kitchen, work long hours, and remain calm and focused in the face of adversity. A chef's ability to balance artistry and efficiency is paramount, as they must be able to produce stunning dishes while keeping pace with the frenzied rhythm of a kitchen.

The life of a chef is one of constant exploration, discovery, and refinement. They are always on the lookout for new ingredients, techniques, and culinary trends, honing their skills and expanding their repertoire. A chef's legacy is built upon their creations, which leave a lasting impression on the taste buds and memories of their diners.

Chefs are at the forefront of a culinary revolution, which is rapidly transforming the way we eat and perceive food. With a spirit of innovation and a commitment to excellence, chefs can push the boundaries of taste, nourish the body and soul, and inspire a new generation of culinary artists to carry on their legacy.

CHEMIST

Chemists are scientists who specialize in the study of matter and its properties. They investigate the composition and behavior of substances at the atomic and molecular level. With their expertise in chemistry, they work to develop new materials, drugs, and technologies that can improve our world.

Chemists study a range of topics, from the structure of atoms and molecules to the chemical reactions that occur when these substances interact. They apply this knowledge to a variety of fields, including medicine, engineering, materials science, and environmental science. Chemists may work in a laboratory setting, conducting experiments and analyzing data, or they may work in the field, studying natural systems and collecting samples.

One of the most important applications of chemistry is in the development of new drugs and medicines. Chemists work to identify and isolate natural compounds that have the potential to be used in medical treatments, and then modify these compounds to enhance their effectiveness and safety. Chemists also study the effects of drugs on the human body, including how they are absorbed, distributed, and metabolized.

Another important area of chemistry is materials science. Chemists work to develop new materials with specific properties, such as strength, flexibility, and conductivity. They also study the properties of existing materials, including metals, polymers, and ceramics, and develop ways to improve them. For example, chemists may work on developing new types of plastics that are more biodegradable, or better metals more resistant to corrosion.

Environmental chemistry is another important field, with chemists working to understand the chemical processes that occur in natural systems. They study how chemicals interact with the environment, and work to develop methods for monitoring and reducing pollution. This includes developing methods for cleaning up contaminated soil and water, and developing new technologies for producing energy in a more sustainable way.

As with most scientific fields, technology plays an important role in the work of chemists. They use advanced tools and instruments to study the properties of matter at a very small scale. For example, they may use electron microscopes to study the structure of atoms, or they may use spectroscopy to study the absorption and emission of light by different substances.

Chemists must also be skilled communicators, as they often work on collaborative teams with other scientists, engineers, technicians and even policymakers to educate them about the potential benefits and risks of different chemical technologies.

CHIROPRACTOR

Chiropractors are health professionals who specialize in diagnosing and treating problems with the musculoskeletal system, especially the spine. They believe that the nervous system is closely related to the spine and that any misalignment of the spine can cause a wide range of health problems. Chiropractors use various non-invasive techniques to help patients manage pain, improve their mobility, and restore their overall health.

One of the most important tools of the chiropractor is the adjustment, or manipulation, of the spine. This involves using their hands or special instruments to apply a controlled force to a joint, moving it beyond its normal range of motion. This is done to relieve pressure and pain in the joint and to restore normal functioning. Chiropractors also use other manual techniques, such as massage, to help loosen up tight muscles and improve range of motion.

Chiropractors treat a wide range of conditions related to the musculoskeletal system, such as back pain, neck pain, headaches, and joint pain. They also treat injuries related to sports or other physical activities. Chiropractors take a holistic approach to healthcare, which means they look at the entire body to determine the root cause of a patient's problems. They consider the patient's lifestyle, nutrition, and exercise habits to develop a treatment plan that is tailored to the patient's individual needs.

Chiropractors also provide education and advice to their patients. They teach their patients how to improve their posture and how to prevent injuries in the future. They may also recommend exercises or stretches to improve flexibility and strength. Chiropractors are also skilled at providing lifestyle counseling, such as nutritional advice, stress management, and smoking cessation.

To become a chiropractor, one must complete a four-year doctoral program, which includes both classroom study and hands-on clinical experience. Chiropractors are licensed by their state regulatory boards, which ensure that they meet the highest standards of education and practice.

Chiropractors have a very rewarding career, as they are able to help people improve their quality of life without the use of drugs or surgery. They work in a variety of settings, such as private practices, hospitals, and clinics. They are also able to work with people of all ages, from newborns to the elderly.

CHOCOLATIER

A chocolatier is a confectionery artist who masterfully sculpts and paints with the medium of chocolate, crafting exquisite and enchanting creations that captivate the senses and indulge the soul. These passionate professionals are the alchemists of the culinary world, transforming humble cacao beans into delectable treats that delight the palate, uplift the spirit, and weave a spell of sweet enchantment.

The journey of a chocolatier begins with a profound appreciation for the rich, complex, and versatile nature of chocolate. They immerse themselves in the study of cacao, exploring its origins, cultivation, and processing, as well as the myriad flavors, textures, and melting points that distinguish different types and blends. Armed with this knowledge, the chocolatier embarks on a creative odyssey, inventing and refining recipes, techniques, and designs that showcase the full potential of this beloved ingredient.

Chocolatiers work in a variety of settings, from cozy artisanal boutiques and bustling confectionery factories to luxurious hotels and world-class culinary schools. They may specialize in a particular style or technique, such as handcrafted truffles, intricate molded chocolates, or avant-garde chocolate sculptures. Regardless of their niche, all chocolatiers share a common goal: to elevate the art of chocolate-making to new heights and inspire wonder and joy in their customers.

To flourish as a chocolatier, one must possess a unique blend of skills and qualities, such as artistic vision, attention to detail, patience, and a finely tuned palate. Chocolatiers must also be adept at working with temperature-sensitive materials and maintaining strict standards of hygiene and quality. Many chocolatiers acquire their craft through formal culinary training, apprenticeships, or self-guided exploration, honing their skills through years of practice, experimentation, and refinement.

The life of a chocolatier is a sensory symphony, filled with the enticing aromas, velvety textures, and sublime flavors of chocolate in all its forms. They are always seeking new ways to push the boundaries of their craft, whether by incorporating exotic ingredients, pioneering innovative techniques, or exploring the intersection of chocolate and other culinary arts. A chocolatier's creations are more than mere confections; they are edible masterpieces that evoke memories, awaken emotions, and transport the senses to realms of pure indulgence.

CITY PLANNER

A city planner, also known as an urban planner, plays an essential role in shaping the physical and social development of a city. They are responsible for designing, developing, and managing a city's infrastructure, such as transportation, housing, and public spaces.

City planners work to improve the quality of life for residents by ensuring that the urban environment is functional, sustainable, and visually appealing. They consider a wide range of factors, including population growth, transportation systems, housing needs, and environmental concerns, when developing plans for a city's future.

One of the key tasks of a city planner is to develop comprehensive land-use plans that guide how land is developed and used. This process involves analyzing population growth, economic trends, transportation patterns, and environmental factors, among other things. The resulting plan outlines the specific actions that need to be taken to ensure that the city can grow in a sustainable and functional way.

Another important aspect of a city planner's job is to work with local communities to ensure that their needs and concerns are taken into account in the planning process. This involves engaging with residents, community groups, and other stakeholders to gain a better understanding of their needs and concerns.

City planners also play a crucial role in designing transportation systems that meet the needs of a growing population. This includes planning the placement of roads, highways, public transit systems, bike lanes, and pedestrian walkways. They also consider the environmental impact of transportation systems and work to find ways to reduce traffic congestion and air pollution.

In addition to designing transportation systems, city planners are also responsible for developing public spaces such as parks, recreational areas, and cultural centers.

The work of a city planner requires a strong background in urban planning, as well as skills in project management, communication, and problem-solving. City planners work closely with other professionals such as architects, engineers, and landscape designers, as well as government officials and community groups.

City planning can be a highly rewarding career for those who are passionate about designing sustainable, livable, and beautiful urban environments.

Did you know that city planning was an Olympic competition in the four Olympic games between 1928 and 1948?

CIVIL ENGINEER

Civil engineers are responsible for designing, building, and maintaining the infrastructure that surrounds us every day. This includes buildings, roads, bridges, tunnels, airports, water treatment facilities, and much more. Civil engineers are involved in every step of the construction process, from planning and design to construction and maintenance.

One of the most exciting things about being a civil engineer is the ability to design and build things that have a positive impact on people's lives. For example, a civil engineer might design a new bridge that helps people travel more efficiently, or they might design a new water treatment plant that provides clean drinking water to a community.

To become a civil engineer, you will need to have a strong foundation in math and science. You will need to take courses in subjects like calculus, physics, and chemistry, as well as courses in civil engineering-specific subjects like mechanics, materials, and structures. In addition, you will need to develop strong problem-solving and critical thinking skills, as these are critical to being a successful civil engineer.

Civil engineers work in a variety of settings, from construction sites to offices to laboratories. They might spend time outside inspecting a construction site, or they might work in an office using computer programs to design buildings and infrastructure.

One of the most important skills for a civil engineer is the ability to work as part of a team. Civil engineering projects are complex and require input from many different professionals, including architects, construction workers, and government officials.

Some specific tasks that a civil engineer might be responsible for include:

- Planning and designing new construction projects, such as bridges and highways
- Analyzing data, such as soil samples, traffic patterns, and environmental reports
- Monitoring and testing materials used in construction, such as concrete and steel, to ensure that they meet safety and quality standards

In summary, civil engineering is a profession that allows you to make a real difference in the world by designing and building infrastructure that has a positive impact on people's lives. If you have a passion for math, science, and problem-solving, and are interested in designing and building the world around us, then a career in civil engineering might be the perfect fit for you!

COMMERCIAL PILOT

A commercial pilot is a navigator of the skies, deftly guiding awe-inspiring flying machines across vast expanses of Earth's atmosphere, connecting people, places, and cultures in the blink of an eye. These intrepid professionals are the guardians of the airways, entrusted with the immense responsibility of safely transporting passengers and cargo to their destinations while delivering an unparalleled experience of human flight. Commercial pilots work for airlines, cargo companies, or private aviation companies, and they often fly large, commercial aircraft such as Boeing 737s or Airbus A320s.

Commercial pilots have a lot of responsibilities, and it all starts before they even step into the cockpit. Pilots must go through rigorous training and education to earn their license to fly commercial aircraft. This includes classroom learning, flight simulators, and many hours of flight time under the supervision of experienced pilots. Once they have completed their training and earned their license, they must pass regular medical and proficiency exams to ensure they are fit to fly.

One of the most important responsibilities of a commercial pilot is to ensure the safety of their passengers and crew. They must constantly monitor their aircraft's systems, weather conditions, and other factors that could affect the flight. Another important aspect of being a commercial pilot is communication. Pilots must communicate effectively with their co-pilot, flight attendants, air traffic control, and other ground crew to ensure that everyone is on the same page and that the flight is running smoothly.

But being a commercial pilot isn't only about the technical aspects of flying. Pilots must also have good leadership and decision-making skills. In an emergency situation, pilots must make quick and sometimes difficult decisions to ensure the safety of their passengers and crew.

Now, let's talk about what makes being a commercial pilot so exciting and interesting. For one, pilots get to travel to many different places around the world. They might start their day in New York City and end up in London by evening. This kind of travel can be very exciting and rewarding, especially for those who love to see new places and experience new cultures.

Finally, being a commercial pilot can be a very lucrative career. Pilots are highly skilled professionals, and they are in demand all over the world.

COMPUTER PROGRAMMER

A computer programmer is someone who creates software and writes instructions for computers to follow. They are like the architects of the digital world, designing and building the programs that we use every day, from video games to social media apps to online shopping websites.

Computer programming involves writing code, which is a set of instructions that tells the computer what to do. These instructions are written in programming languages, such as Python, Java, or C++, that the computer can understand. A programmer has to be very detail-oriented and logical, and they have to be able to think critically and solve problems creatively.

There are many different types of programming jobs, from creating video games to developing financial software to designing websites. Some programmers work for large companies, while others work for themselves as freelancers or consultants.

To become a programmer, you can start by learning some basic coding skills. There are many online resources and coding courses available, and many schools now offer coding classes as well. You can also practice your programming skills by creating their own simple games or applications, using programming languages like Scratch or Code.org.

As you get more experienced with coding, you can start to explore more advanced programming concepts, like algorithms, data structures, and computer science theory. There are also many programming competitions and hackathons that you can participate in, which can be a fun way to hone your skills and meet other young programmers.

If you are interested in becoming a computer programmer, you should be prepared to work hard and learn constantly. The best programmers are passionate about their work and enjoy the challenge of solving complex problems with code.

In addition to being a rewarding and challenging career, computer programming is also a field with many opportunities for growth and advancement. As technology continues to play a larger role in our lives, the demand for skilled programmers is only going to increase, making it a great field for kids to consider as they think about their future careers.

CONSERVATIONIST

Conservationists are professionals who work to protect and preserve the natural environment and the species that inhabit it. They work to protect and conserve the ecosystems, biodiversity, and natural resources that make our planet habitable for all living organisms.

The main focus of conservationists is to ensure the sustainability of our natural resources by studying and protecting natural habitats, and working towards creating policies and regulations that promote sustainability. They work towards reducing the human impact on the environment, while also balancing the needs of the environment with the needs of society.

There are many different paths that conservationists can take, and each one involves different duties and responsibilities. Some may work in research and data analysis, while others may work on the ground, in the field, to manage and conserve natural habitats.

One of the primary responsibilities of a conservationist is to collect and analyze data about the environment. They may use a variety of tools and technologies, such as geographic information systems (GIS), satellite imagery, and remote sensing to gather information about ecosystems, climate, and natural resources. This information is then used to develop strategies and policies that promote sustainable practices and protect the environment.

Conservationists also work to manage and maintain natural habitats. This may involve removing invasive species, planting native vegetation, and managing water resources to ensure that ecosystems remain healthy and stable. They also work to identify threats to biodiversity and implement measures to protect endangered species.

On top of their scientific and technical skills, conservationists also need to have strong communication skills. They must be able to communicate complex scientific concepts to the public, policymakers, and other stakeholders in a way that is easily understood.

Conservationists may work for a variety of organizations, including government agencies, non-profits, and research institutions. They may also work in a variety of places, such as national parks, wildlife reserves, and private lands.

The work of conservationists is incredibly important for the health and sustainability of our planet. By working to protect and conserve natural resources, they are ensuring that future generations will be able to enjoy and benefit from our planet's unique and diverse ecosystems.

CONSTRUCTION WORKER

Construction workers are the people who build our homes, schools, hospitals, roads, and more. They are the backbone of the construction industry, and they use their skills and expertise to turn blueprints into real-life structures.

A construction worker can work on a variety of different projects. Some might build houses, while others might work on skyscrapers, bridges, or highways. No matter what kind of project they're working on, they all share a few common tasks.

First and foremost, construction workers are responsible for building things. This might mean digging the foundation for a new building, laying down pipes for a new water system, or putting up walls and roofs. They work with a wide range of materials, including wood, concrete, and brick.

Another important part of a construction worker's job is reading and interpreting blueprints. These are detailed plans that show exactly how a building or structure should be built. Construction workers need to be able to read these plans and understand what they mean so that they can build things to the right specifications.

Construction workers also need to be able to use a variety of tools and equipment. This might include hand tools like hammers and saws, power tools like drills and circular saws, and heavy machinery like cranes and bulldozers.

Safety is also a top priority for construction workers. They work in environments that can be dangerous, with heavy machinery and materials that can cause serious injury or even death. That's why construction workers need to follow strict safety procedures and wear protective gear like hard hats, gloves, and safety glasses.

Despite the challenges and risks involved, many people find working in construction to be incredibly rewarding. Seeing a project come together from start to finish can be a deeply satisfying experience, and construction workers get to take pride in the fact that they are building something that will last for generations.

If you're interested in becoming a construction worker, there are a few things you can do to get started. Many construction workers start out as apprentices, which means they work alongside more experienced workers to learn the ropes. Some may also go to vocational schools to learn the skills they need to succeed in the industry.

COPYWRITER

Copywriting is a really cool job, especially if you love writing and you're really creative! A copywriter is someone who writes words to sell products, services, or ideas. They use their writing skills to create messages that will make people want to buy something or take action.

Have you ever seen a commercial on TV, or an ad in a magazine or on a website? That's the work of a copywriter! They use their skills to create catchy slogans, jingles, and other types of content that make you want to learn more about a product or service.

One of the things that makes copywriting so interesting is that there are many different types of copywriters. Some work for big advertising agencies and create ads for big companies. Others work for smaller companies or freelance and write copy for things like websites, brochures, or social media.

The key to being a successful copywriter is to be really good at understanding people. A great copywriter needs to know what motivates people to buy things and how to connect with them on an emotional level. They also need to have great writing skills and be able to write in a way that is easy to understand and engaging.

To become a copywriter, you'll need to start by developing your writing skills. You can practice by writing short stories, poems, or even blog posts. The more you write, the better you'll become!

Once you've developed your writing skills, you'll need to start learning about marketing and advertising. You can do this by taking courses or reading books about marketing, consumer behavior, and advertising. You'll also want to start learning about the different types of copywriting and the different formats used for different types of ads.

One of the most exciting parts of being a copywriter is that you get to work on a variety of projects. One day, you might be creating a TV commercial for a new toy, and the next day, you might be writing social media posts for a new clothing brand. Every day is different and exciting, and you get to use your creativity to help businesses succeed.

Overall, copywriting is a fun and creative job that allows you to use your writing skills to make a difference in the world. If you love writing and you're interested in marketing and advertising, then copywriting might be the perfect career for you!

CORPORATE TRAINER

Have you ever been to a training session at school or in a club, where someone teaches you something new or helps you get better at a skill you already have? Well, a corporate trainer is kind of like that, but for grown-ups in a company or business.

A corporate trainer is a person who helps employees learn new skills or improve their current ones in order to be more effective in their jobs. They might train people on specific software or technology, teach them customer service techniques, or help them improve their public speaking skills, among other things.

One thing that's really cool about being a corporate trainer is that you get to work with people from all different departments in a company, so you're constantly learning about new things and meeting new people. You might work with the sales team one day and the IT department the next day, depending on what kind of training is needed.

To be a good corporate trainer, you need to be a good communicator and a good teacher. You need to be able to explain things clearly and in a way that people can understand. You also need to be patient and understanding, because not everyone learns at the same pace or in the same way.

Another important part of being a corporate trainer is being able to design training programs that are effective and engaging. This means coming up with creative ways to teach people, using games or role-playing exercises to help them learn, and making sure that everyone is engaged and participating.

As a corporate trainer, you might work for a company full-time or you might work as a freelancer and be hired on a project-by-project basis. Either way, you'll need to be comfortable with public speaking and presenting in front of groups of people, since that's a big part of what you'll be doing.

One thing to keep in mind is that being a corporate trainer is a great way to help people and make a positive impact on a company. When you help employees improve their skills and become more effective in their jobs, you're not only helping them, but you're also helping the company be more successful overall.

So, if you enjoy teaching and helping people, and you're interested in corporate environments, becoming a corporate trainer could be a great career path for you!

COSTUME DESIGNER

Costume design is a crucial part of the entertainment industry, from movies to theatre to television. Costume designers are responsible for creating and designing the outfits and costumes that are worn by actors and actresses, and they play a significant role in helping to bring characters to life on screen or stage.

A costume designer's role typically involves reading scripts or briefs and interpreting the requirements for each character or scene. They may work closely with the director, set designer, and makeup artist to ensure that all the elements of a scene complement each other and help to tell the story effectively. They may also research historical, cultural, or regional references to create a costume that accurately reflects the period or location of the piece.

Once the designer has an idea of what the costumes should look like, they will create sketches and work with a team of skilled costume makers to bring their vision to life. They may also work with fabric suppliers to find the perfect materials for each outfit.

In addition to creating costumes, a costume designer may also be responsible for fitting actors and actresses, ensuring that each piece fits correctly and is comfortable to wear. They may also be responsible for coordinating the wardrobe department, which may involve hiring staff and managing budgets.

Costume designers must be creative and have an eye for detail, as well as a strong understanding of fashion, textiles, and design principles. They must also be able to work collaboratively and take direction from directors and producers.

In film and television, costume designers must also be skilled at adapting costumes to accommodate different camera angles and lighting conditions. They must be able to work quickly and efficiently, often under tight deadlines, and be prepared to make last-minute changes to costumes if necessary.

In theatre, costume designers must work closely with the performers to ensure that the costumes are practical and easy to move in. They may also need to design and create costumes that can be changed quickly between scenes or even mid-performance.

The role of a costume designer can be highly rewarding, as their work is often highly visible and has a significant impact on the overall success of a production. A well-designed costume can help to transport audiences to another time and place, and can even become iconic in its own right. Many successful costume designers have gone on to win awards for their work, including Academy Awards for Best Costume Design in film.

CRIMINAL LAWYER

Criminal lawyers are attorneys who specialize in representing clients who have been accused of crimes. They help people who have been charged with criminal offenses, such as robbery, assault, or murder, to navigate the legal system and defend themselves against the accusations.

One of the most important roles of a criminal lawyer is to protect the rights of their clients. They ensure that their clients are not subjected to unfair treatment, such as being questioned without an attorney present, and that their clients' rights are not violated in any way. They also work to ensure that their clients receive a fair trial, by investigating the evidence and arguing their clients' cases in court.

Criminal lawyers work closely with their clients to understand the details of their cases, as well as their clients' concerns and goals. They advise their clients on the best course of action, and help them make decisions about plea bargains, trials, and appeals. They also help their clients understand the legal process and the potential consequences of different actions.

In addition to working with their clients, criminal lawyers also interact with a variety of other professionals in the legal system. They may work with police officers, forensic specialists, and expert witnesses to investigate the evidence and build a strong defense for their clients. They also communicate with judges, prosecutors, and other attorneys in order to negotiate plea bargains, argue their clients' cases, and reach favorable outcomes for their clients.

One important aspect of criminal law is the principle of "innocent until proven guilty." This means that, under the law, a person is considered innocent until the prosecution can prove beyond a reasonable doubt that they committed a crime. Criminal lawyers are responsible for making sure that their clients are treated fairly and not subjected to unfounded accusations or convictions.

Criminal lawyers must also be knowledgeable about the legal system, including criminal law and court procedures. They must stay up-to-date with changes in the law and be able to apply their knowledge to different cases. They must also be skilled at analyzing evidence and presenting arguments in court, both orally and in writing.

CRYPTOGRAPHER

A cryptographer is someone who specializes in making and breaking codes and ciphers. They use mathematical concepts and computer algorithms to create and decipher secret messages. Cryptography is an ancient art, with evidence of codes and ciphers being used by ancient civilizations such as the Greeks and the Egyptians. Today, cryptographers work in a variety of fields, from national security to online banking.

At its most basic level, cryptography is the art of writing or solving codes. For example, imagine you want to send a secret message to someone, but you don't want anyone else to be able to read it. You could use a code that only you and the recipient know how to decipher. For instance, you could assign a number to each letter of the alphabet and then use those numbers to represent each letter in your message. This is a simple code, but it can be effective if it's kept secret.

However, modern cryptography is much more complex than simple substitution ciphers. Cryptographers today use advanced mathematical algorithms and computer software to create much more secure codes that are much harder to crack. They work in a variety of fields, from cybersecurity to national defense. Cryptographers also play a critical role in the development of cryptocurrencies like Bitcoin, which rely on complex algorithms to ensure the security of transactions.

One of the most famous examples of cryptography is the Enigma machine used by the German military during World War II. The Enigma machine was a complex device that used a series of rotors to scramble messages. The Germans believed that the Enigma machine was unbreakable, but a team of cryptographers working for the Allies managed to crack the code and gain access to German military communications.

In addition to creating codes and ciphers, cryptographers also work to break them. Cryptanalysis is the study of how to break codes and ciphers, and cryptanalysts use a variety of techniques to try to crack encrypted messages. This can involve everything from statistical analysis to brute-force attacks, where a computer tries every possible key until it finds the right one.

Cryptographers work in a variety of fields, from national defense to cybersecurity. They are employed by governments, banks, and private companies to help protect sensitive information. Cryptography is also used in many everyday applications, from secure online transactions to the encryption of email messages.

Cryptographers are at the forefront of developing new technologies to keep information safe and secure, and their work plays an increasingly important role in our digital world.

CUSTOMER SERVICE REPRESENTATIVE

A customer service representative, also known as a customer support specialist, is someone who works for a company to help customers with any questions or issues they may have. This person is often the first point of contact for customers who need help, and they can be found working in a variety of industries, such as retail, technology, healthcare, and more.

One of the main responsibilities of a customer service representative is to listen to customers and understand their needs. This can involve answering questions about products or services, helping customers place orders, or resolving complaints. A good customer service representative is patient and empathetic, and they work hard to make sure that every customer feels heard and valued.

Customer service representatives use a variety of tools and techniques to help customers. They may use phone, email, or live chat to communicate with customers, and they often have access to a company's database or knowledge base to help answer questions. They may also work with other teams within the company, such as technical support or product development, to find solutions to complex customer issues.

In addition to helping customers, customer service representatives are also responsible for keeping accurate records of customer interactions. This can include logging phone calls, chat transcripts, or other forms of communication. By keeping detailed records, a customer service representative can help ensure that a customer's needs are addressed quickly and efficiently.

To become a customer service representative, it is important to have excellent communication skills and a friendly, outgoing personality. A customer service representative should be comfortable working with people from all walks of life, and should be able to work well under pressure. Many companies offer on-the-job training for customer service representatives, but some may also require formal education or certification.

While the job of a customer service representative can be challenging, it can also be very satisfying. Helping people solve problems and providing excellent customer service can make a real difference in people's lives, and it can be a great way to build strong relationships with customers and colleagues alike.

CYBERSECURITY ANALYST

Have you ever heard of the term "cybersecurity"? It's all about protecting computers, networks, and information from bad guys who want to steal or damage them. And a cybersecurity analyst is one of the people who helps keep these things safe!

Basically, a cybersecurity analyst is like a detective. They investigate the digital world to find out if there are any threats to a company's computer systems. They use their skills to identify and prevent cyberattacks and keep important information secure.

So, what exactly does a cybersecurity analyst do? Some of their responsibilities are:

- Identifying and assessing cyber threats: This is where the detective work comes in. Cybersecurity analysts use special software and tools to detect any suspicious activity on a computer network. They also look for any vulnerabilities that hackers might be able to exploit.
- Developing and implementing security measures: Once they identify a threat, cybersecurity analysts work with other experts to come up with a plan to stop it. This might involve developing new software to protect against viruses or setting up firewalls to keep out intruders. They also make sure that employees are following best practices for keeping data safe, like using strong passwords and not sharing sensitive information.
- Monitoring systems: Even after security measures are in place, cybersecurity analysts continue to watch over computer networks to make sure that everything is running smoothly. They keep an eye out for any signs of a breach, and quickly respond if they detect anything suspicious.
- Investigating incidents: Sometimes, despite the best efforts of cybersecurity analysts, a breach occurs. In these cases, cybersecurity analysts work to identify the source of the breach, figure out what information has been compromised, and take steps to prevent it from happening again in the future.

As you can see, being a cybersecurity analyst involves a lot of detective work. It also requires a strong understanding of computer networks and programming, as well as knowledge of the latest cybersecurity threats and trends. If you're interested in becoming a cybersecurity analyst you can study computer science and programming in school, and work on developing your problem-solving and analytical skills.

DATA ANALYST

A data analyst is someone who uses their knowledge of mathematics, statistics, and computer science to analyze large amounts of data and extract useful insights from it. They work with data from various sources, such as surveys, customer records, and web traffic, and use tools like Excel, SQL, and Python to organize, clean, and manipulate the data in preparation for analysis.

Once the data is ready, the data analyst uses statistical techniques and machine learning algorithms to identify patterns, trends, and relationships in the data. They then present their findings in a clear and concise manner, often using graphs, charts, and other visual aids.

Data analysts work in a variety of industries, including healthcare, finance, marketing, and technology. They may focus on specific areas of analysis, such as market research or business operations, or they may have a broader role in analyzing data across the entire organization.

One exciting aspect of being a data analyst is the ability to work with cutting-edge technologies, such as big data platforms and artificial intelligence. Data analysts are often at the forefront of developing new tools and techniques for analyzing data, which means they get to be part of an innovative and ever-evolving field.

For kids who are interested in becoming a data analyst, it's important to have a strong foundation in math and computer science. They should also be curious and detail-oriented, with a love for solving puzzles and finding patterns. A good data analyst also needs to be an effective communicator, able to explain complex concepts in a way that is easy for others to understand.

In addition to technical skills, data analysts also need to be creative and adaptable. They need to be able to think outside the box and come up with innovative solutions to complex problems. They also need to be comfortable working with uncertainty and ambiguity, as data analysis is rarely a straightforward process.

Overall, being a data analyst can be a challenging and rewarding career path, with plenty of opportunities for growth and development. It's a great choice for kids who love math, science, and technology, and who want to use their skills to make a real impact in the world.

DELIVERY DRIVER

Delivery drivers are the unsung heroes of the modern world. They are the people who work hard to make sure that packages and goods are delivered to their destinations on time. They are responsible for the safe and timely delivery of everything from pizza to packages.

Imagine you're sitting at home, ordering some food online. You place the order and wait patiently for it to arrive. That's where the delivery driver comes in. They pick up your order from the restaurant or store, and then drive it to your house. They make sure that your food is hot and ready to eat when it arrives.

Delivery drivers work for all kinds of companies, from local restaurants and grocery stores to large online retailers like Amazon. They use a variety of vehicles, such as cars, trucks, and vans, to deliver goods to customers. Some delivery drivers even ride bikes or use scooters to get around.

The job of a delivery driver is more than just driving. They also have to be good at customer service. They need to be friendly and professional when they arrive at the customer's location, and make sure that the customer is satisfied with their order.

One of the biggest challenges of being a delivery driver is managing time. They have to make sure that they get to each location on time, even if there's traffic or bad weather. They also need to make sure that they have enough time to deliver all the orders they need to in a single day.

Another challenge is staying organized. Delivery drivers have to keep track of multiple orders at once, and make sure that they don't forget anything. They need to be able to navigate different areas and find their way around unfamiliar neighborhoods.

Despite these challenges, being a delivery driver can be a rewarding job. You get to work independently, and you get to see a lot of different places. You also get to interact with different types of people, which can be a great experience.

In conclusion, delivery drivers are a crucial part of our modern economy. They are responsible for the timely and safe delivery of goods, and they work hard to make sure that customers are satisfied with their orders.

DENTAL HYGIENIST

Dental hygienists play a vital role in preventing and treating dental diseases. As a dental hygienist, you'll become an expert in oral care, mastering the art of cleaning teeth and removing plaque and tartar that can lead to tooth decay and gum disease. You'll wield specialized instruments, like ultrasonic scalers and curettes, with the precision and skill of a fine artist, sculpting and polishing teeth to perfection.

But there's more to this fascinating career than cleaning teeth. Dental hygienists are also educators and advisors, empowering patients to take control of their oral health. You'll impart your wisdom on proper brushing and flossing techniques, as well as provide guidance on nutrition and lifestyle choices that can impact dental health. By sharing your knowledge, you'll help patients develop healthy habits and prevent future dental problems, making a lasting impact on their lives.

One of the most appealing aspects of becoming a dental hygienist is the opportunity to form meaningful connections with patients. You'll see familiar faces returning for regular checkups and cleanings, and you'll play an essential role in their healthcare journey. As you build trust and rapport, you'll watch your patients grow – from children learning the importance of oral hygiene to adults maintaining their dental health as they age.

Dental hygienists are also detectives, examining patients' mouths for signs of gum disease, oral cancer, and other conditions that may require further attention. With your keen eye and expertise, you'll be able to identify potential issues early, ensuring that your patients receive timely care and treatment. In this way, you'll contribute to the early detection and prevention of serious health problems, further solidifying the importance of your role in the healthcare team.

In the realm of dental hygiene, you'll have the chance to develop an array of valuable skills, such as radiography. You'll learn how to take dental X-rays, which are crucial diagnostic tools that reveal hidden issues beneath the surface of teeth and gums.

As a dental hygienist, you'll have the opportunity to work in various settings, such as private dental practices, public health clinics, hospitals, and educational institutions. This versatility offers you the freedom to choose a work environment that aligns with your values, interests, and career goals. Furthermore, the demand for dental hygienists is expected to grow, providing you with job stability and promising career prospects.

DENTIST

Dentistry is a rewarding profession that revolves around the diagnosis, prevention, and treatment of oral health issues. Dentists play a crucial role in promoting dental hygiene and ensuring the well-being of their patients' teeth and gums. By working in this field, professionals contribute to their patients' overall health, boost their self-confidence, and improve their quality of life.

To become a dentist, one typically needs to complete a bachelor's degree, followed by dental school, which takes around four years. Dental school entails a mixture of classroom instruction, lab work, and clinical experience, where aspiring dentists get hands-on training under the guidance of experienced professionals. After dental school, individuals must pass a licensing exam to practice dentistry in their respective regions.

Dentists can choose to specialize in various areas, such as pediatric dentistry, orthodontics, periodontics, endodontics, or oral surgery. Each specialization requires additional training and education, but it allows professionals to focus on specific aspects of dentistry that interest them the most.

One fascinating aspect of dentistry is the use of advanced technologies, such as digital X-rays, 3D imaging, and computer-aided design (CAD) systems. These tools enable dentists to diagnose and treat dental issues with greater accuracy and precision, improving patient outcomes. For example, CAD technology can help dentists create custom crowns, bridges, and other dental restorations with remarkable precision, ensuring a perfect fit.

An interesting example of a dentist's work is the treatment of a young patient with a severe overbite, which can lead to difficulties in speech, chewing, and self-esteem. After conducting a thorough examination and evaluating the patient's medical history, the dentist might recommend orthodontic treatment involving braces, retainers, or other corrective devices. Over time, these appliances help to gradually shift the teeth and jaw into proper alignment, significantly improving the patient's bite and appearance.

A career in dentistry offers several benefits, including a stable income, flexible work hours, and the opportunity to make a meaningful impact on people's lives. Dentists can choose to work in private practices, hospitals, community health centers, or educational institutions. As dental care continues to advance, dentists remain at the forefront of promoting oral health and enhancing the lives of their patients.

DERMATOLOGIST

Dermatologists are doctors who specialize in the treatment of the skin, hair, and nails. They are experts in diagnosing and treating conditions that affect the skin, including acne, eczema, psoriasis, warts, and skin cancer. If you have ever had a skin condition, chances are you have seen a dermatologist.

Dermatologists work in a variety of settings, including hospitals, clinics, and private practice. They see patients of all ages, from babies to the elderly. Many dermatologists also conduct research and teach medical students.

Dermatologists spend a lot of time examining patients' skin, hair, and nails to look for any abnormalities or signs of disease. They may use special tools like magnifying glasses, bright lights, and even special cameras that can take detailed images of the skin. They also take into account a patient's medical history, as well as any symptoms they may be experiencing.

Once a dermatologist has made a diagnosis, they will work with the patient to develop a treatment plan. This may involve prescribing medication, performing a procedure, or recommending lifestyle changes. For example, a dermatologist may prescribe a topical cream for acne, perform a mole removal surgery, or suggest changes to a patient's diet or skincare routine.

Dermatologists also perform a variety of cosmetic procedures, such as Botox injections, chemical peels, and laser treatments. These procedures can help patients achieve a more youthful and vibrant appearance.

One of the most important parts of a dermatologist's job is educating patients about their skin health. They may teach patients how to properly care for their skin, how to avoid sun damage, and how to detect signs of skin cancer. By helping patients take better care of their skin, dermatologists can prevent many skin conditions from developing in the first place.

Becoming a dermatologist requires many years of education and training. Like all doctors, dermatologists must complete a bachelor's degree, medical school, and a residency program. In addition, they must pass a rigorous board certification exam. However, the hard work and dedication pays off in the end, as dermatology is a rewarding and fulfilling career that helps people look and feel their best.

DESIGNER

Designers are creative professionals who use their imagination, technical skills, and artistic abilities to create designs that can be used in a variety of fields such as graphic design, web design, fashion, interior design, and more. They have a passion for making things look visually appealing and they use their creativity to create designs that communicate messages and solve problems.

Graphic designers use their artistic abilities and software tools to create visual designs that communicate a message. They design logos, websites, business cards, packaging, billboards, and more. They also use typography, color, and layout to create visually appealing designs that can help a company or organization stand out.

Web designers create websites that are easy to navigate and visually appealing. They design the layout, colors, and graphics for websites, making sure that they are user-friendly and responsive across multiple devices. They also create wireframes and prototypes to test how users interact with the website and make adjustments accordingly.

Fashion designers create clothing and accessories that are fashionable and functional. They use their creative abilities to design clothing that is both stylish and practical. They sketch designs, choose fabrics and colors, and create patterns that can be used to create a final product. They work with manufacturers and fashion houses to bring their designs to life.

Interior designers use their artistic skills to create functional and aesthetically pleasing spaces. They work with clients to create designs that are tailored to their needs and style. They use color, texture, and lighting to create a space that is inviting and functional. They also work with contractors to ensure that their designs are implemented correctly.

Regardless of the type of designer, all designers need to be creative, detail-oriented, and have a good sense of style. They also need to have excellent communication skills, as they will be working with clients and other professionals in their field. In addition, they must stay up to date with the latest design trends and software tools.

Becoming a designer requires a combination of creativity, technical skills, and education. Many designers have a bachelor's degree in design or a related field, but some successful designers are self-taught. There are also many workshops, conferences, and online tutorials available for aspiring designers to hone their skills.

DJ

A disc jockey, more commonly known as a DJ, is an entertainer responsible for selecting and playing recorded music for audiences at various events and venues. DJs not only create the perfect atmosphere for parties, weddings, nightclubs, and festivals, but also showcase their creativity and passion for music. This dynamic profession combines technical skills, musical knowledge, and the ability to read a crowd, making it an exciting and fulfilling career path for music enthusiasts.

To become a DJ, there is no specific educational requirement. However, many DJs acquire their skills through self-study, online tutorials, workshops, or mentorships. An aspiring DJ may start by learning the fundamentals of music theory, beatmatching, and mixing techniques, as well as familiarizing themselves with various DJ equipment, such as turntables, mixers, and digital software.

In recent years, digital technology has transformed the world of DJing, with tools like digital vinyl systems and DJ software enabling professionals to perform intricate mixes were once impossible using traditional equipment. This evolution has opened up new creative possibilities for DJs to develop their unique style and stand out in the industry.

An interesting example of a DJ's work might involve performing at a themed event, such as a 1980s dance party. The DJ would meticulously curate a playlist featuring iconic hits from the era, seamlessly blending tracks to maintain a high-energy atmosphere and keep the dance floor packed. Throughout the night, the DJ must skillfully adapt to the crowd's energy, adjusting their song selection and mixing techniques to ensure the audience remains engaged and entertained.

Beyond live performances, DJs may also pursue careers in radio broadcasting, where they host shows, curate playlists, and engage with listeners on-air. This aspect of DJing allows professionals to share their love for music with a broader audience.

A career as a DJ offers the opportunity to follow one's passion for music, travel to various locations, and connect with diverse audiences. DJs can work as freelancers or under the umbrella of entertainment agencies or event management companies. While the income in this profession can be unpredictable, especially at the beginning, DJs with a strong reputation and unique style can achieve financial success and enjoy a thrilling, creative career.

DOCTOR

A medical doctor, or physician, is a respected professional who diagnoses, treats, and prevents various illnesses and injuries in patients. They play an essential role in maintaining public health, improving patients' quality of life, and providing compassionate care. This rewarding career path offers the opportunity to make a meaningful impact on individuals while enjoying a stable income and intellectual growth.

To become a medical doctor, one must first complete a bachelor's degree, typically with a focus on pre-medical or science-related coursework. Following their undergraduate education, aspiring doctors attend medical school, which usually takes four years. The first two years of medical school consist of foundational coursework in subjects like anatomy, physiology, and pharmacology, while the latter half emphasizes hands-on clinical experience under the supervision of licensed physicians.

After medical school, graduates must complete a residency program in their chosen specialty. Residency programs typically last between three to seven years, depending on the specialty, and provide in-depth training and experience in various aspects of patient care. Doctors can specialize in a wide variety of fields, such as family medicine, internal medicine, surgery, pediatrics, obstetrics and gynecology, or psychiatry, among others.

A compelling example of a medical doctor's work might involve an orthopedic surgeon treating a patient with severe knee pain due to osteoarthritis. After taking an in-depth medical history and performing a comprehensive physical examination, the surgeon would order diagnostic tests, such as X-rays or MRIs, to determine the extent of joint damage. If conservative treatments like physical therapy, pain-relief medications, and lifestyle modifications prove insufficient, the surgeon might propose a total knee replacement surgery.

In addition to diagnosing and treating patients, doctors often engage in research, contribute to medical literature, and participate in continuing education to stay current with advancements in their field.

A career as a medical doctor requires dedication, resilience, and empathy, but it offers immense satisfaction in improving patients' lives and contributing to the greater good. As healthcare continues to evolve, medical doctors remain at the forefront, ensuring the well-being of individuals and communities around the world.

ECONOMIST

An economist is someone who studies how people make choices and how society uses resources like land, labor, and capital to produce goods and services. They use this knowledge to help governments, businesses, and individuals make decisions about everything from pricing goods and services to setting economic policies.

Economists are like detectives who try to understand how the economy works by gathering and analyzing data. They use math, statistics, and computer programs to make sense of information about the economy, such as employment rates, inflation, and consumer spending.

One of the most important things economists study is the concept of supply and demand. This refers to how much of a product or service is available (supply) and how much people want it (demand). When demand is high and supply is low, prices tend to go up, and when supply is high and demand is low, prices tend to go down. Economists use this information to help businesses decide how much to produce and how much to charge for their goods and services.

Economists also study how people and businesses spend their money, and how government policies affect the economy. For example, if the government decides to cut taxes, economists can predict how this will impact consumer spending and business investment. Similarly, if a country is experiencing high inflation, economists can recommend policies to combat it.

One interesting area of economics is behavioral economics, which looks at how people make decisions based on their emotions, social pressures, and other factors besides pure rationality. Behavioral economists study things like why people make certain financial choices, such as investing in the stock market or buying a certain product.

Economists work in a variety of settings, including government agencies, non-profit organizations, research firms, and financial institutions. They often work in teams with other economists, as well as with experts from other fields such as finance, and statistics.

If you're interested in becoming an economist, it's important to have strong analytical and critical thinking skills, as well as a solid foundation in math and statistics. You'll also need to be able to communicate your findings and recommendations clearly and effectively, both in writing and verbally.

ELECTRICAL ENGINEER

Electrical engineers are the masterminds behind some of the most important technologies that we use every day, from the computer or phone you're reading this on to the electrical systems that keep your home and community running. If you're interested in how things work, love technology, and enjoy solving problems, becoming an electrical engineer might be the perfect career for you!

So, what exactly does an electrical engineer do? Put simply, an electrical engineer designs, develops, tests, and supervises the manufacturing of electrical equipment and systems. Electrical engineers can work in a variety of fields, including telecommunications, power generation, and transportation.

One of the primary responsibilities of an electrical engineer is to design new systems and equipment. This involves using computer-aided design (CAD) software to create blueprints and schematics for circuits, components, and systems. Electrical engineers must have a deep understanding of physics and mathematics to be able to create and test complex designs.

Once a design is complete, electrical engineers oversee the manufacturing and testing of the equipment. This can involve working closely with technicians and other engineers to ensure that the equipment is built according to the specifications in the blueprint.

In addition to designing and testing equipment, electrical engineers are often responsible for maintaining and improving existing electrical systems. This can include things like power grids, telecommunications networks, and transportation systems. Electrical engineers must be able to troubleshoot and repair complex systems quickly and efficiently to prevent interruptions in service.

Electrical engineers also play an important role in developing new technologies. They are constantly researching and experimenting to find new ways to use electrical power more efficiently and effectively. This can involve developing new materials, improving existing technology, or even creating entirely new types of technology.

Finally, electrical engineers must also be able to communicate effectively with others, including clients, technicians, and other engineers. They must be able to explain complex technical information in a way that is easy to understand for people without an engineering background.

ELECTRICIAN

Electricians are skilled tradespeople who work with electrical systems. They install, maintain, and repair electrical wiring, lighting, and control systems in homes, businesses, and other structures. Electricians play a crucial role in ensuring that people have access to safe, reliable electricity.

Electricians work on a wide range of electrical systems, from simple residential wiring to complex industrial machinery. They must have a thorough understanding of electrical theory and the National Electrical Code (NEC) to ensure that all work is done safely and up to code. This means that electricians must have a high degree of attention to detail, as even small mistakes can be dangerous.

One of the most important tasks of an electrician is to ensure that electrical systems are safe. This involves identifying potential safety hazards, such as exposed wires or overloaded circuits, and taking steps to mitigate these risks. Electricians must also be skilled at troubleshooting electrical problems, using a combination of their knowledge of electrical theory and their experience in the field to diagnose and fix issues.

In addition to safety and troubleshooting, electricians also install and maintain electrical systems. This can include everything from wiring a new building to installing lighting fixtures and control systems. Electricians may work on new construction projects, or they may be called in to upgrade or repair existing electrical systems.

There are many different types of electricians, each with their own specializations. Some electricians focus on residential work, while others specialize in commercial or industrial applications. There are also electricians who work specifically on renewable energy systems, such as solar or wind power.

Electricians use a wide range of tools in their work, from simple hand tools like wire cutters and pliers to more specialized equipment like multimeters and oscilloscopes. They may also use power tools like drills and saws, as well as heavy machinery like backhoes.

Becoming an electrician requires a combination of education and hands-on experience. Most electricians start by completing an apprenticeship program, which involves both classroom instruction and on-the-job training. Apprenticeships typically last four, and after that, electricians must pass a licensing exam to become a licensed electrician.

EPIDEMIOLOGIST

Epidemiologists are public health professionals who study the patterns, causes, and effects of diseases in populations. They work to prevent the spread of infectious diseases and to reduce the risk of chronic illnesses. In a world that has recently experienced the COVID-19 pandemic, the work of epidemiologists has become more important than ever.

Epidemiologists use a range of methods to gather and analyze data, including surveys, interviews, and laboratory tests. They also work closely with medical professionals and community organizations to gather information about diseases and public health issues.

One of the primary tasks of epidemiologists is to investigate outbreaks of disease. When a new illness is identified, epidemiologists work to identify the source of the outbreak and determine the best way to contain it. This may involve interviewing people who have been infected, testing environmental samples, or tracing the movements of people who have been exposed to the disease.

Epidemiologists also work to prevent the spread of diseases through public health interventions. This may involve working with health care providers to promote vaccination or other preventive measures, or providing education to the public about how to protect themselves from infectious diseases.

Another important aspect of epidemiology is the study of risk factors for diseases. Epidemiologists look at the factors that contribute to the development of illnesses, such as genetics, lifestyle, and environmental exposures. They use this information to develop strategies for reducing the risk of illness in the population.

Epidemiologists work in a range of settings, including government agencies, hospitals, research institutions, and community organizations. They may specialize in a particular area of public health, such as infectious disease, chronic disease, or environmental health.

One of the most interesting aspects of epidemiology is the use of data to make predictions about future disease outbreaks. Epidemiologists use statistical models to analyze data and predict the likelihood of future outbreaks.

The work of epidemiologists is essential to protecting public health, and it is a rewarding career for people who are interested in making a difference in the lives of others. If you're interested in pursuing a career in epidemiology, there are a range of educational paths available. Many epidemiologists have a master's degree in public health or a related field, but there are also opportunities to enter the field with a bachelor's degree or through on-the-job training.

ETHICAL HACKER

An ethical hacker, also known as a "white hat" hacker, is a cybersecurity expert who uses their skills to find weaknesses in computer systems and networks, in order to identify and fix vulnerabilities before they can be exploited by malicious actors. These professionals are hired by companies and organizations to conduct security tests and assessments, with the ultimate goal of preventing cyber-attacks and data breaches.

One of the most important roles of an ethical hacker is to simulate real-world cyber-attacks in a controlled environment, such as a test network or virtual machine. By using a variety of techniques and tools, such as penetration testing, vulnerability scanning, and social engineering, ethical hackers attempt to breach the security of a target system in order to identify weaknesses and develop strategies for improving its defenses.

Unlike malicious hackers, ethical hackers use their skills and knowledge for good, and always obtain permission before attempting to access any systems or data. They work closely with IT and security teams to understand the architecture of the systems they are testing, and collaborate with developers and engineers to design and implement solutions to any issues that are identified.

Another important aspect of an ethical hacker's work is staying up to date with the latest trends and techniques in cybersecurity. Because the field is constantly evolving and new threats emerge every day, ethical hackers must be able to adapt and learn quickly in order to keep their skills sharp and maintain their effectiveness.

There are a number of different types of ethical hackers, each with their own specialties and areas of expertise. Some focus on network security, while others specialize in web application security, mobile device security, or cloud security. Others may specialize in specific industries, such as healthcare or finance, and work to identify vulnerabilities and develop customized solutions to protect against cyber threats.

Ethical hackers are an important part of the cybersecurity landscape, working to keep systems and data safe from cyber-attacks and other security threats. For kids who are interested in technology and problem-solving, a career as an ethical hacker can be an exciting and rewarding path to pursue.

EVENT PLANNER

Do you remember the last time you went to a birthday party or a wedding and everything was perfect? The decorations were amazing, the music was just right, and the food was delicious. You probably didn't realize it at the time, but someone was behind the scenes making sure everything went smoothly - that person was an event planner.

An event planner is someone who plans and coordinates events of all kinds, from small birthday parties to large conferences and weddings. They work with clients to understand their vision and make it a reality. To become an event planner, you need to have great organizational skills, be creative, and be able to work well under pressure.

One of the first things an event planner does is to meet with the client to get an understanding of what they want for their event. They might ask questions such as the theme, the number of guests, the type of food they want to serve, and the overall ambiance they want to create. Once the event planner has a clear understanding of the client's vision, they begin to make arrangements for the event.

This includes finding the perfect location for the event, whether it's a hotel, conference center, or someone's home. They also need to hire vendors for things like catering, music, and decorations. The event planner needs to make sure that all the details are taken care of, from coordinating with the venue to ensure proper setup and layout to scheduling deliveries and making sure everything is in place before the guests arrive.

One of the most important roles of an event planner is to make sure the event runs smoothly. They are responsible for ensuring everything happens on time and that all the vendors know what they need to do. They also troubleshoot any issues that may arise during the event, such as a late delivery or a guest who has a special request.

In addition to planning the event itself, an event planner is also responsible for managing the budget. They work with the client to determine how much they want to spend and then work to make sure everything stays within that budget. This means negotiating with vendors for the best prices and finding creative solutions to keep costs down without sacrificing quality.

Event planning can be a very rewarding career, but it requires a lot of hard work and dedication. Event planners often work long hours, especially leading up to an event, and need to be able to handle stressful situations with grace and professionalism.

EXECUTIVE ASSISTANT

An executive assistant is a highly skilled and trusted professional who offers administrative support to high-level executives such as CEOs, presidents, and other top-level managers. Executive assistants are often called the "right-hand" of their executives because they help their bosses with a wide range of tasks, including managing schedules, arranging travel, preparing reports, and coordinating meetings.

At its core, an executive assistant's job is to help their executive run the business as smoothly as possible. They do this by taking care of all the administrative details so that the executive can focus on the big picture. This can involve anything from managing the executive's calendar to handling incoming phone calls and emails, and making sure the office is running smoothly.

One of the most important parts of an executive assistant's job is to be able to communicate effectively. They need to be able to take a wide range of information and distill it down into clear and concise reports that their executive can quickly and easily understand. They also need to be able to communicate with people at all levels of the company, from other executives to lower-level staff members and customers.

Another important part of an executive assistant's job is to be able to stay organized and on top of things. They need to be able to manage multiple tasks and priorities simultaneously, and to be able to switch gears quickly as needed. They also need to be able to anticipate their executive's needs and take proactive steps to address them, rather than waiting for instructions.

In addition to administrative duties, executive assistants are often involved in strategic planning and decision-making. They may be responsible for researching and analyzing data, developing and implementing new policies and procedures, and managing special projects.

To be successful as an executive assistant, it is important to have strong organizational and communication skills, as well as a high level of professionalism and discretion. You will need to be able to handle sensitive and confidential information, and to be able to work effectively with people from all walks of life. You will also need to be adaptable and able to work in a fast-paced, dynamic environment where priorities can change quickly.

FARMER

Farming is a vital profession that has been around for thousands of years. Farmers are responsible for growing crops, raising livestock, and managing land to produce food and other products that support our daily lives. They play a crucial role in maintaining the food supply chain and ensuring that we have access to fresh and nutritious food.

The daily life of a farmer can vary depending on the type of farming they do, the size of their farm, and the location. However, there are several tasks that most farmers perform on a regular basis. For example, they might wake up before sunrise to feed and care for their livestock or inspect their crops. They might spend their mornings repairing equipment, tending to their animals, or planting new crops. Afternoons might be spent watering, weeding, or harvesting crops, while evenings might be spent cleaning up, managing finances, or planning for the next day.

One of the most important tasks of a farmer is managing their crops. This involves selecting the right seeds, preparing the soil, planting the crops, and ensuring that they receive the right amount of water, nutrients, and sunlight to grow properly. Farmers must also monitor the weather and make adjustments to their crops to ensure that they are protected from extreme heat, cold, wind, or rain.

Another key aspect of farming is animal care. Farmers who raise livestock must ensure that their animals are healthy, well-fed, and protected from disease. They might spend hours each day feeding, watering, and cleaning up after their animals, as well as providing medical care when needed. They also need to manage breeding and herd health to ensure the quality of their animals and the sustainability of their operation.

In addition to growing crops and raising animals, farmers also need to manage the business side of their operation. This includes marketing their products, managing their finances, and making decisions about which crops to grow or which livestock to raise based on market demand. They might also need to negotiate with suppliers and distributors, and work with government agencies to obtain permits or comply with regulations.

To be successful in their profession, farmers need to have a wide range of skills and knowledge. They need to be able to operate and maintain various types of farm equipment, including tractors, plows, and combines. They also need to have a strong understanding of soil science, animal husbandry, and plant biology. Communication and marketing skills are also important, as farmers need to be able to sell their products and negotiate with suppliers and distributors.

FASHION DESIGNER

Fashion designers are creative professionals who create new designs and styles for clothing, shoes, and accessories. They use their artistic and technical skills to produce unique and innovative designs that are both functional and aesthetically pleasing.

To become a fashion designer, you must have a strong sense of style and a keen eye for detail. You must also be able to keep up with the latest fashion trends, and be able to combine your own personal style with the needs and desires of your clients or target market.

Fashion designers start by sketching their ideas and concepts for new clothing lines or collections. They then create patterns and prototypes for their designs, often using a variety of fabrics and materials to test the look and feel of the garments. Once the final designs have been selected, fashion designers oversee the manufacturing process to ensure that the finished products are of the highest quality.

In addition to designing clothing, fashion designers must also be skilled in marketing and promotion. They must know how to create a brand identity and build a loyal customer base, and must be able to work with photographers, models, and other professionals to showcase their products in fashion shows and other events.

To succeed as a fashion designer, you must be able to work well under pressure and meet tight deadlines. You must be able to handle criticism and rejection, as not all of your designs will be successful or well-received. You must also be willing to take risks and experiment with new materials, techniques, and styles.

Fashion designers can work in a variety of settings, from high-end fashion houses and design studios to small boutiques and independent design firms. They may also work in related industries such as textile manufacturing, retail sales, or fashion journalism.

Overall, being a fashion designer is a challenging and rewarding career that requires a great deal of creativity, dedication, and hard work. If you have a passion for fashion and are willing to put in the time and effort required to succeed, then a career as a fashion designer may be the perfect fit for you.

FILM DIRECTOR

A film director is a captivating storyteller, a magician who conjures up entire worlds on screen, crafting unforgettable experiences that resonate with audiences worldwide. The career path of a film director is an adrenaline-pumping adventure filled with twists and turns.

The journey begins with an unquenchable passion for storytelling. Aspiring directors often enroll in film schools, where they learn the intricacies of storytelling, cinematography, editing, and sound design. They take their first steps into the realm of cinema, armed with the knowledge and skills to bring their stories to life.

Emerging from the cocoon of film school, the fledgling director embarks on a series of creative explorations. Short films, music videos, and commercials offer opportunities to hone their skills, develop their unique voice, and showcase their talent. Christopher Nolan, for example, started with a low-budget independent film, "Following," which laid the groundwork for his mind-bending masterpieces like "Inception" and "Interstellar."

As the director ascends the ladder of success, networking and self-promotion become crucial. Film festivals serve as launching pads for their careers, providing opportunities to connect with industry professionals. Quentin Tarantino's "Reservoir Dogs" premiered at Sundance Film Festival, catapulting him to fame and leading to iconic films like "Pulp Fiction" and "Kill Bill."

The director's ascent continues as they enter the world of feature films or television series. A reputation for visionary storytelling can lead to a breakthrough project that defines their career. Consider Patty Jenkins, who shattered box office records and societal norms with "Wonder Woman," becoming a beacon for female directors in a male-dominated industry.

Navigating the unpredictable landscape of filmmaking, directors face artistic, technical, and financial challenges. Each project is a collaborative puzzle, solved in conjunction with writers, cinematographers, actors, and producers. The director becomes the anchor, balancing creative vision with the realities of filmmaking.

The life of a film director is a thrilling saga of triumphs, challenges, and dreams brought to life. It demands passion, resilience, and an unwavering love for the art of storytelling. Ultimately, the director stands tall as a master of their craft, with the power to captivate, inspire, and move the hearts of millions.

FINANCIAL ADVISOR

Financial advisors are specialists who work with clients to help them manage their money and achieve their financial goals. These goals can range from planning for retirement, paying off debt, buying a home, starting a business, or simply building wealth.

A financial advisor's primary goal is to provide their clients with personalized advice and guidance on how to manage their finances. This can include investment advice, tax planning, retirement planning, estate planning, risk management, and more. They help clients create a financial plan that is tailored to their specific goals and needs.

Financial advisors can work in a variety of settings, including banks, investment firms, and independent firms. They may work with individual clients, small businesses, or large corporations. They typically have a strong understanding of financial markets, investment products, and financial planning strategies.

Some of the key responsibilities of a financial advisor include:

1. Building relationships with clients: Financial advisors need to build strong relationships with their clients in order to understand their unique needs and goals.

2. Assessing financial situations: A financial advisor must analyze a client's current financial situation, including their income, expenses, debts, assets, and investments. This helps them to identify areas where the client may need to make changes in order to achieve their financial goals.

3. Developing financial plans: Once the financial advisor has a thorough understanding of a client's financial situation and goals, they can develop a customized financial plan. This may include investment strategies, retirement planning, tax planning, and other financial goals.

4. Monitoring investments: A financial advisor is responsible for monitoring their clients' investments and adjusting their portfolios as needed. This requires a deep understanding of financial markets and investment products.

To become a financial advisor, you typically need a bachelor's degree in finance, accounting, or a related field. Some financial advisors also hold advanced degrees, such as a master's degree in finance or an MBA. They may also need to obtain professional certifications, such as a Certified Financial Planner (CFP) or a Chartered Financial Analyst (CFA) designation.

FINANCIAL ANALYST

Financial analysts are professionals who use their expertise to make sense of complex financial information and help individuals and organizations make smart investment decisions. They help investors understand the performance and health of a company, providing valuable insight into the inner workings of a business.

As a financial analyst, you might work for an investment firm, a bank, a corporation, or a government agency. Your job would be to help your employer or clients make sound financial decisions by analyzing data and providing informed recommendations. You would typically use a combination of financial and economic data, market trends, and industry knowledge to help clients make smart investment choices.

One of the key responsibilities of a financial analyst is to evaluate the financial performance of a company. This involves analyzing a variety of financial statements, including income statements, balance sheets, and cash flow statements, to determine how well a company is performing. You might also assess a company's financial health by looking at key financial ratios, such as debt-to-equity ratios and return on equity.

You might follow market trends and perform market research to help clients identify potential investment opportunities. This could involve conducting in-depth research on specific companies or industries, as well as analyzing market and economic data to help forecast future trends.

To be successful as a financial analyst, you need to have a strong foundation in finance, accounting, and economics, as well as a deep understanding of financial markets and investment strategies. You should also possess excellent analytical and critical thinking skills, as well as strong communication and presentation skills.

While financial analysts typically work in office settings, the job can be fast-paced and demanding. You may be required to work long hours, especially during peak market periods, and must be able to manage multiple tasks and projects simultaneously.

In summary, financial analysts play an essential role in the investment industry, helping individuals and organizations make smart financial decisions. Their expertise and analytical skills help provide valuable insight into the inner workings of businesses and financial markets, making them essential to the financial success of individuals and companies alike.

FIREFIGHTER

Firefighters are courageous and highly trained individuals who are responsible for responding to emergency situations involving fires, hazardous materials, natural disasters, and other emergency situations that threaten people, property, and the environment. They are one of the most respected and essential groups of professionals in any community, putting their lives on the line to protect and serve others.

The primary responsibility of firefighters is to respond to emergencies involving fires, as well as rescue people and pets from dangerous situations. They are the first responders to the scene, and their primary objective is to contain and extinguish the fire as quickly and safely as possible. They also ensure that the area is safe and secure for the public and other emergency responders.

Firefighters work in a team environment and use specialized equipment and tools to control and extinguish fires. They may use hoses, ladders, axes, and other tools to gain access to the fire and to create openings for ventilation. They may also use chainsaws, thermal imaging cameras, and other specialized equipment to locate and extinguish hot spots and hidden fires.

In addition to firefighting duties, firefighters are also trained to respond to other emergency situations. They may respond to hazardous materials spills, natural disasters such as earthquakes, floods, and tornadoes, and rescue situations such as water rescues and vehicle extrications.

One of the most important roles of firefighters is to prevent fires and educate the public about fire safety. They provide educational programs and conduct safety inspections to help prevent fires from occurring in the first place.

Firefighters must be physically fit and mentally prepared to handle the rigors of the job. They must be able to work under stressful and dangerous conditions, often in extreme heat and smoke. They must also be able to work in teams and follow established protocols to ensure everyone's safety.

To become a firefighter, one must first complete the required education and training. This typically includes completing a high school diploma or GED, obtaining an EMT or paramedic certification, and attending a fire academy to receive training in firefighting, rescue operations, hazardous materials, and other emergency response skills.

FISHERMAN

A fisherman is a professional who harvests fish and other aquatic organisms from various bodies of water, such as oceans, lakes, and rivers. This timeless occupation is not only essential for providing a vital food source to communities around the world but also contributes to local and global economies. A career as a fisherman combines physical endurance, skill, and a deep connection with nature, offering a unique and adventurous lifestyle for those who are passionate about the outdoors.

Fishermen utilize a wide range of fishing methods, depending on the target species, location, and available resources. These methods can include trawling, longlining, seine netting, or even traditional techniques like spearfishing or handlining. Adept fishermen continuously adapt their strategies in response to environmental conditions, fish populations, and regulatory requirements, ensuring that their practices remain sustainable and productive.

An interesting example of a fisherman's work might involve harvesting wild salmon during the peak of their annual migration. The fisherman would rely on their knowledge of the salmon's migratory patterns, local waterways, and seasonal weather conditions to select the optimal fishing location and technique. By employing sustainable methods, such as using appropriately sized nets or hooks, the fisherman can harvest salmon while minimizing the impact on other aquatic species and ecosystems.

To become a fisherman, no formal education is typically required. However, aspiring fishermen can benefit from training programs, apprenticeships, or on-the-job experience to learn essential skills, such as boat handling, navigation, and fishing techniques.

Fishermen can work independently, as part of a crew on a larger fishing vessel, or as members of a fishing cooperative. Their work schedule is often dictated by factors such as weather, seasonal availability of fish, and local regulations. As a result, a fisherman's income can be unpredictable, and the job may require long hours and extended periods away from home.

Despite the challenges, a career as a fisherman offers the opportunity to work in nature, engage with local communities, and contribute to the sustainable management of vital aquatic resources. Fishermen play a crucial role in the global food supply chain and can take pride in their profession's rich cultural and economic significance.

FITNESS TRAINER

A fitness trainer, also known as a personal trainer, is a professional who helps clients reach their fitness goals by designing and implementing workout programs tailored to their needs. Fitness trainers work with individuals or groups, either in-person or online, to help them improve their strength, endurance, flexibility, and overall fitness.

Fitness trainers often begin by meeting with clients to assess their current fitness levels, discuss their goals, and identify any health concerns or limitations that may impact their workout program. Based on this information, the trainer designs a custom workout plan that may include cardiovascular exercises, strength training, flexibility exercises, and other activities to help clients achieve their goals.

One of the most interesting aspects of the fitness trainer profession is the wide range of clients they work with. They may work with individuals of all ages, from teenagers who want to improve their sports performance, to seniors who want to maintain their mobility and independence.

Another interesting aspect of the profession is the variety of settings in which fitness trainers work. Some trainers work in gyms or fitness centers, while others work in clients' homes or outdoors in parks and other public spaces.

In addition to designing workout programs, fitness trainers also play an important role in educating their clients about exercise and healthy lifestyle habits. They may provide guidance on nutrition, stress management, and other factors that impact overall health and wellness. This educational component of the job is important for helping clients make sustainable lifestyle changes that can improve their overall well-being.

Another interesting aspect of the fitness trainer profession is the creativity and problem-solving skills required to design effective workout programs. Trainers must be able to tailor workouts to their clients' unique needs and preferences, while also adapting to any physical limitations or injuries. This requires a deep understanding of human anatomy and physiology, as well as the ability to think creatively and adjust workouts on the fly.

Fitness trainers must also have strong communication skills to effectively motivate and engage their clients. This involves more than just barking orders or counting reps – trainers must be able to listen to their clients, understand their needs and motivations, and provide positive feedback and encouragement to keep them on track.

FLIGHT ATTENDANT

A flight attendant is a someone who is responsible for ensuring the safety, comfort, and well-being of passengers on board commercial flights. This dynamic career path provides the opportunity to travel the world, interact with diverse cultures, and make a positive impact on the lives of countless travelers. Flight attendants must possess excellent communication skills, a customer service mindset, and the ability to handle high-pressure situations with grace and poise.

Flight attendants play a crucial role in maintaining safety on board an aircraft. They are responsible for demonstrating safety procedures before each flight, monitoring passengers to ensure compliance with regulations, and assisting during emergencies. In addition to safety duties, flight attendants are also responsible for addressing passengers' needs and concerns, and creating a welcoming and comfortable atmosphere on the flight.

To become a flight attendant, candidates must typically have a high school diploma or equivalent, although some airlines may prefer candidates with a college degree or previous experience in customer service. Aspiring flight attendants must also complete a specialized training program, usually provided by the airline, which covers topics such as safety procedures, emergency response, first aid, and customer service techniques.

An intriguing example of a flight attendant's work could involve managing a medical emergency during a long-haul flight. Upon discovering a passenger having trouble breathing, the flight attendant would quickly assess the situation and coordinate with the pilots to contact medical professionals on the ground for guidance. Simultaneously, the flight attendant would administer first aid, such as providing oxygen and ensuring the passenger's comfort, until the plane could safely land and the individual could receive further medical attention.

Flight attendants often work irregular schedules, including nights, weekends, and holidays, due to the round-the-clock nature of air travel. Their work environment can be physically demanding, with long hours on their feet and frequent travel across different time zones. However, the career also offers unique perks, such as discounted or free travel, along with the chance to explore the world during layovers.

Flight attendants play a vital role in the airline industry, ensuring that passengers reach their destinations safely and with a memorable experience.

FLORIST

Florists are the professionals who specialize in working with flowers and plants to create beautiful arrangements for various occasions, including weddings, funerals, birthdays, and more. They also work with clients to create custom arrangements that suit their specific needs and preferences.

One of the main tasks of a florist is to source and select the right flowers and plants for each occasion. This requires an in-depth knowledge of different types of flowers and plants, including their growing seasons, colors, and meanings. They need to have a good understanding of which flowers complement each other well and how to create arrangements that are both visually pleasing and long-lasting.

Once the florist has selected the flowers and plants, they then use their creativity to arrange them in unique and beautiful ways. This involves cutting, trimming, and shaping the flowers and plants to create the desired effect. Florists also use various techniques to add visual interest and texture to their arrangements, such as adding ribbons, decorative vases, or other decorative elements.

In addition to creating beautiful arrangements, florists are responsible for maintaining the quality of the flowers and plants they work with. This includes keeping the flowers fresh and alive, ensuring that they are properly watered, and making sure that they are kept in the right temperature and lighting conditions. They also need to be aware of potential problems such as pests or diseases that could damage the plants.

To become a successful florist, it is important to have a combination of artistic skills and knowledge of horticulture. A background in botany, landscape design, or a related field can be helpful, but many florists gain their skills through hands-on experience and training. Most florists begin their careers working for established flower shops, where they can learn from experienced florists and gain valuable on-the-job training.

In addition to their technical skills, successful florists also need to be good communicators and have strong customer service skills. They need to be able to work closely with clients to understand their specific needs and preferences, and to offer helpful suggestions and advice when necessary. They must also be able to work under pressure, especially during peak seasons like Valentine's Day and Mother's Day.

FOOD CRITIC

A food critic is a professional who is responsible for assessing the quality of food and drink in restaurants, cafes, bars, and other eateries. They typically work for newspapers, magazines, or online publications, and their reviews and ratings can have a significant impact on a restaurant's reputation and success. One of the most well-known and prestigious guides for restaurants is the Michelin Guide, which has been published since 1900 and is considered the ultimate authority on the best dining experiences in the world.

Food critics are passionate about food and drink and are always on the lookout for new and exciting dining experiences. They visit restaurants anonymously, paying close attention to everything from the quality of the ingredients to the presentation of the dishes. They also evaluate the service, atmosphere, and overall dining experience.

One of the most important aspects of a food critic's job is to provide honest and objective feedback about their dining experiences. They must be able to communicate their impressions in a way that is informative, insightful, and engaging for their readers. Food critics must also be knowledgeable about different cuisines, culinary techniques, and the latest food trends.

The Michelin Guide is the most prestigious restaurant guide in the world, with its origins in France in the early 20th century. It originally provided information to motorists about where to find good food and accommodation during their travels. Today, the guide covers restaurants in 32 countries, with a team of anonymous inspectors who visit restaurants and rate them on a scale of one to three stars.

A Michelin-starred restaurant is considered the pinnacle of culinary excellence, and chefs and restaurateurs aspire to earn a coveted Michelin star or two. One Michelin star is a mark of very good cuisine, two stars indicate excellent cooking that is worth a detour, and three stars mean exceptional cuisine that is worth a special journey.

Food critics who write for the Michelin Guide are among the most influential in the industry. They are passionate about food and drink and have a deep knowledge of the culinary arts. They visit restaurants anonymously and pay attention to every detail, from the quality of the ingredients to the presentation of the dishes. They evaluate the service, atmosphere, and overall dining experience and provide objective feedback to their readers.

In addition to writing reviews, food critics may also write articles, cookbooks, and other content related to food and drink. They may attend food and wine events, participate in cooking demonstrations, and collaborate with chefs and restaurateurs on projects.

FOOD SCIENTIST

A food scientist is a professional who studies food and the various chemical, biological, and physical processes that occur during the production, processing, packaging, and storage of food. They work to develop and improve food products, and to ensure that these products are safe, nutritious, and of high quality.

To become a food scientist, you need a solid understanding of food science and technology, as well as a good foundation in chemistry, biology, and physics. You may need a degree in food science, chemistry, or a related field, as well as some experience working in the food industry.

One of the most interesting aspects of being a food scientist is the opportunity to work on developing new food products. Food scientists use their knowledge of chemistry and biology to understand the properties of different ingredients, and to develop new recipes and techniques for creating food products that are nutritious, tasty, and visually appealing.

Food scientists also work to improve the quality and safety of existing food products. They may conduct research to identify the causes of food spoilage, develop methods for detecting and preventing foodborne illnesses, and work with food companies to implement new safety procedures and protocols.

Another interesting aspect of being a food scientist is the opportunity to work on developing sustainable food production methods. Food scientists work to develop new techniques for growing crops and raising livestock that are environmentally friendly and reduce waste.

Food scientists also play an important role in ensuring that food products meet regulatory requirements and industry standards. They may work with government agencies to develop and enforce food safety regulations, and they may work with food companies to ensure that their products meet quality and safety standards.

One of the most challenging aspects of being a food scientist is working with a wide range of food ingredients and processing techniques. Food scientists must be able to understand the chemical and physical properties of different ingredients, and they must be able to develop and implement new processing methods that maintain the quality and safety of the final product.

FOREIGN LANGUAGE INTERPRETER

A foreign language interpreter is a skilled professional who facilitates communication between individuals or groups speaking different languages. This vital role enables cross-cultural exchanges, empowers international cooperation, and breaks down language barriers in various settings, such as business meetings, conferences, legal proceedings, and medical appointments. A career as a foreign language interpreter requires linguistic proficiency, cultural sensitivity, and the ability to think quickly and accurately under pressure.

To become a foreign language interpreter, one must first achieve a high level of fluency in at least two languages, including their native tongue. Many interpreters hold a bachelor's degree in a foreign language, linguistics, or a related field, although some professionals acquire their skills through immersion in a foreign country or intensive language programs. Additionally, specialized training or certification programs, such as those offered by professional organizations or universities, can enhance an interpreter's skills and credibility.

A curious example of a foreign language interpreter's work might involve interpreting at a high-stakes diplomatic summit between two countries. The interpreter would need to accurately and impartially convey the nuances of each speaker's message, ensuring that both parties can communicate effectively and reach mutual understanding. In this context, the interpreter's role is crucial for fostering international collaboration and potentially shaping the course of global events.

The demand for skilled foreign language interpreters is expected to grow, particularly in areas such as healthcare, law, and international relations. Technological advancements, such as remote interpreting platforms, have further expanded the interpreter's reach, allowing them to provide services to clients around the world without leaving their home office.

A career as a foreign language interpreter offers the chance to make a significant impact on people's lives, bridge cultural divides, and contribute to global understanding. Interpreters not only facilitate communication but also foster empathy and collaboration, playing an indispensable role in an increasingly interconnected world.

FORENSIC SCIENTIST

Forensic science is the application of scientific principles and techniques to the investigation of crimes and other legal disputes. A forensic scientist is a highly trained professional who is responsible for analyzing and interpreting physical evidence in order to determine its relevance to a criminal investigation.

Forensic scientists are involved in a wide range of investigations, from the most basic to the most complex. They may be called upon to analyze anything from a single hair or fiber to the entire crime scene, using a variety of tools and techniques to examine and collect evidence.

One of the most important roles of a forensic scientist is to analyze and interpret physical evidence. This can include anything from DNA samples to bloodstains, fingerprints, and bullet fragments. In order to do this, forensic scientists use a wide range of tools and techniques, including microscopy, chromatography, and spectroscopy.

Forensic scientists also play an important role in the collection and preservation of physical evidence. They are responsible for making sure that the evidence is properly collected, packaged, and stored, in order to prevent contamination and to ensure that the evidence is admissible in court.

In addition to their work in the lab, forensic scientists are often called upon to testify in court as expert witnesses. They may be asked to explain their findings to a judge and jury, and to help them understand the significance of the evidence in a particular case.

Forensic science is a highly specialized field, and forensic scientists may specialize in a particular area of investigation, such as DNA analysis, ballistics, or fingerprint analysis. Some forensic scientists work in a laboratory setting, while others may work in the field, collecting and analyzing evidence at crime scenes.

One of the most interesting aspects of forensic science is the way in which it is constantly evolving. As new technologies and techniques are developed, forensic scientists must adapt and learn new skills in order to stay at the forefront of their field. This can include everything from learning how to use new software programs to analyzing evidence in new and innovative ways.

Forensic science can be a highly rewarding career, as forensic scientists play a critical role in the justice system and in helping to bring criminals to justice. However, it can also be a highly challenging career, requiring a high degree of attention to detail, analytical thinking, and the ability to work under pressure.

FREELANCE PROFESSIONAL

A freelance professional is someone who provides specialized services to clients on a project basis, rather than working as a full-time employee for a single employer. Freelance professionals can work in a wide range of industries and offer a variety of services, such as writing, design, programming, accounting, and consulting.

One of the most appealing aspects of being a freelance professional is the freedom to work on a wide range of projects and with a diverse set of clients. Freelancers can often choose to work on projects that are of interest to them, or with clients who share their values or vision. This allows for a high degree of flexibility and creativity in the work they take on.

Another interesting aspect of being a freelance professional is the ability to work from anywhere with an internet connection. This means that freelancers can work from home, from a coworking space, or while traveling. This flexibility can be especially appealing to those who value work-life balance and the ability to manage their own schedules.

Freelancers also have the opportunity to develop their own unique brands and to market their services in a way that reflects their values and expertise. This can be an exciting and empowering aspect of the freelance lifestyle, as it allows professionals to define their own career paths and to build their reputations in their chosen industries.

However, being a successful freelance professional also requires a great deal of discipline and self-motivation. Freelancers need to be able to manage their own time, meet deadlines, and find their own clients. They also need to be able to handle rejection and criticism, and to continuously improve their skills and knowledge in order to stay competitive in their industries.

In addition, freelance professionals need to have a good understanding of the business side of their work. This includes negotiating contracts and rates, managing finances and taxes, and building a strong personal brand and professional network.

Despite these challenges, being a freelance professional can be a rewarding and fulfilling career path for those who value creativity, flexibility, and autonomy. Freelancers have the opportunity to develop their skills and expertise in a way that aligns with their personal and professional goals, and to make a meaningful impact in their chosen industries.

FRONT-END DEVELOPER

A front-end developer is a creative and technical professional who designs and implements the visual and interactive components of websites and web applications. These experts ensure that users have a seamless, engaging, and visually appealing experience when navigating online platforms. A career as a front-end developer combines artistic flair, problem-solving skills, and a strong foundation in coding, making it an exciting choice for those interested in both design and technology.

To become a front-end developer, one typically needs to acquire knowledge in essential web technologies, such as HTML, CSS, and JavaScript. Many professionals hold a degree in computer science, web development, or a related field, but others learn through self-study, or coding bootcamps. Building a diverse and impressive portfolio of projects is crucial for showcasing skills and attracting potential employers or clients.

Front-end developers collaborate closely with web designers, back-end developers, and other team members to create cohesive and user-friendly websites or applications. They take design concepts or mock-ups and transform them into functional, responsive, and visually appealing interfaces.

An interesting example of a front-end developer's work might involve designing an online store for a small business. The developer would create an intuitive layout, ensuring that customers can easily browse products, add items to their shopping cart, and proceed through the checkout process without confusion. By incorporating visually appealing design elements, smooth navigation, and responsive features, the front-end developer would contribute to a positive user experience and, ultimately, the success of the store.

Front-end developers can work in diverse industries, as most organizations require an online presence to connect with their customers or users. They can find employment at web development agencies, technology companies, or even large corporations in non-tech sectors.

The demand for skilled front-end developers is expected to grow, as more businesses and organizations recognize the importance of a polished online presence. Additionally, advances in web development frameworks and tools continue to shape the field, providing front-end developers with new opportunities to create innovative and immersive online experiences.

FULL-STACK DEVELOPER

Full-stack developers are software engineers who work with both the front-end and back-end of web applications. They handle the development, maintenance, and testing of web applications, as well as their deployment and management. In order to accomplish this, they need to have a broad range of technical skills, including expertise in web development languages, database management, and server-side technologies.

One of the most important tasks that a full-stack developer will undertake is to design and implement the user interface of a web application. This requires a deep understanding of web development languages such as HTML, CSS, and JavaScript, as well as an understanding of how to use these languages to create a visually appealing and intuitive user experience. They will also work closely with designers to ensure that the overall look and feel of the application is in line with the brand identity and user experience goals.

In addition to their front-end development work, full-stack developers are also responsible for the back-end of web applications. This includes the server-side scripting and programming that allows a web application to function properly. They need to be familiar with a range of server-side technologies such as Ruby on Rails, Python, and Node.js. They also need to be able to work with databases and be familiar with database management systems such as MySQL and MongoDB.

Another key aspect of the work of a full-stack developer is testing and debugging. They need to be able to test the application for bugs and make sure that it is functioning properly. They also need to be able to troubleshoot and fix any issues that arise in the application. This requires a strong understanding of software development processes and the ability to work on a team to ensure that the application is functioning properly.

Full-stack developer also need to have great communication skills to be able to collaborate effectively with other developers and stakeholders. They will often work in cross-functional teams that include designers, other developers, project managers, and other stakeholders.

One of the biggest benefits of a career as a full-stack developer is the high demand for skilled professionals in this field. As the use of web applications continues to grow, the demand for full-stack developers is expected to continue to rise. This means that there are many exciting opportunities for professionals in this field, including opportunities to work on cutting-edge projects and to work with some of the most innovative companies in the tech industry.

FUNDRAISER

A fundraiser is a dedicated professional who plans, organizes, and oversees campaigns to raise money for various causes, organizations, or projects. They play a crucial role in securing the financial resources needed to support charitable initiatives, educational institutions, healthcare facilities, or even political campaigns. A career as a fundraiser combines strong interpersonal skills, strategic thinking, and a passion for making a positive impact on the world.

Real examples of a fundraiser's work might involve:

- Planning a charity gala to raise funds for a local children's hospital.

- Securing sponsorships, selling tickets, and coordinating with vendors to create an unforgettable event.

- Combining a memorable evening with a heartfelt message about the hospital's mission, inspiring attendees to make generous donations.

Fundraisers can work in various settings, including nonprofit organizations, educational institutions, healthcare facilities, and political campaigns.

They may be employed directly by the organization they support or work as consultants for multiple clients. The role often requires a flexible schedule, as fundraisers may need to attend meetings or events during evenings and weekends to connect with donors and supporters.

As organizations continue to rely on donations and financial support to achieve their goals, the demand for skilled fundraisers is expected to grow. Those who excel in this field can enjoy the satisfaction of knowing that their efforts are directly contributing to meaningful change in their communities and beyond.

In summary, a career as a fundraiser offers the opportunity to blend relationship-building, creativity, and strategic thinking to make a tangible impact on causes and organizations one is passionate about. By inspiring generosity in others, fundraisers play an essential role in empowering positive change and improving lives around the world.

FURNITURE MAKER

A furniture maker is someone who designs, builds, and repairs furniture. They use a variety of tools and materials to create custom pieces that can be used in homes, offices, and other spaces. Furniture makers may work for large furniture companies, small shops, or independently as freelance artisans.

The work of a furniture maker can be very exciting, especially for kids who love to work with their hands and enjoy creating things. Furniture makers get to work with a wide range of materials, including wood, metal, fabric, and leather. They use many different tools, such as saws, drills, hammers, and chisels, to create their designs.

One of the most important skills that furniture makers have is the ability to read and interpret blueprints and design plans. They work closely with clients to understand their needs and preferences, and then create sketches and drawings of the piece they plan to build. These sketches serve as a roadmap for the furniture maker as they work on the project.

In addition to designing and building furniture, furniture makers also need to have a strong understanding of the materials they work with. They need to know how to select the right type of wood or metal for a particular piece, as well as how to treat and finish the material to ensure it lasts a long time. They may also need to be familiar with upholstery techniques if they are making furniture with fabric.

While some furniture makers work in large factories, many work in small shops or even out of their own homes. This can be a very rewarding career path for kids who are interested in working for themselves and being their own boss. However, it's important to note that furniture making can be physically demanding work, as furniture makers spend a lot of time on their feet and may need to lift heavy objects.

One of the most exciting aspects of being a furniture maker is the ability to create custom pieces that are unique and one-of-a-kind. Furniture makers work with their clients to create pieces that fit their specific needs and style preferences. This can range from large dining room tables to smaller pieces like jewelry boxes or bookshelves.

In addition to designing and building furniture, many furniture makers also offer repair and restoration services. They may be called upon to fix a broken leg on a chair, replace a worn-out cushion, or refinish an antique piece. These skills require a deep understanding of furniture construction and the ability to work with precision and attention to detail.

GAME DESIGNER

Have you ever played a video game and thought about how much fun it would be to create your own? Well, that's exactly what game designers do! Game designers are responsible for coming up with the ideas and concepts that turn into the video games we love to play.

Game design is a fascinating blend of creativity, technical skills, and storytelling. Game designers need to have a deep understanding of what makes games fun and engaging, and they also need to have a solid grasp of computer programming, 3D modeling, and graphic design.

Game designers work with a team of artists, programmers, and producers to create new games. They start by coming up with the basic concept for the game, which can include the game's storyline, characters, and setting. They then work with the team to develop the game mechanics, or the rules that govern how the game is played.

Once the game mechanics are in place, the game designer works with the team to create the game's world. This can involve creating 3D models of characters and environments, designing user interfaces, and developing the game's sound effects and music.

As the game takes shape, the game designer is responsible for testing and fine-tuning the gameplay. They work closely with the programming team to make sure that the game is running smoothly and that it is fun to play. They also work with the producers to make sure that the game is on schedule and on budget.

Game designers need to have a wide range of skills and knowledge to succeed in their field. They need to be creative, imaginative, and able to think outside the box. They also need to have strong communication skills, as they will be working closely with a team of other professionals. In addition, they need to have a deep understanding of computer programming, game engines, and software development.

If you're interested in becoming a game designer, there are a number of paths you can take. Many game designers start by studying computer science, graphic design, or animation in college. Others start by creating their own games as a hobby and build up a portfolio of work that they can show to potential employers.

Game design is an exciting and rewarding career, and it's a great way to combine your love of technology with your creative passions. So, if you have a passion for games and a desire to create your own worlds, game design may be the perfect career for you!

GENERAL PRACTITIONER

A general practitioner, or GP, is a medical doctor who provides primary care to patients. They are typically the first point of contact for people seeking medical attention and are responsible for diagnosing and treating a wide range of illnesses and injuries. GPs are a vital part of the healthcare system and play an important role in keeping their communities healthy.

To become a GP, one must first complete a degree in medicine, followed by a period of residency and further training. GPs have a broad range of medical knowledge and are able to provide care for patients of all ages, from infants to the elderly.

One of the most important roles of a GP is to provide preventive care. This involves working with patients to help them maintain good health and prevent illness. This may include providing advice on healthy lifestyle choices, such as diet and exercise, and performing routine check-ups and health screenings.

GPs are also responsible for diagnosing and treating a wide range of illnesses and injuries. They are often the first point of contact for patients who are experiencing symptoms of a health problem. GPs use their medical knowledge and diagnostic skills to determine the underlying cause of the problem and develop a treatment plan.

GPs also provide ongoing care for patients with chronic conditions, such as diabetes or heart disease. They work with patients to develop a management plan that helps them to control their symptoms and improve their quality of life. This may involve prescribing medications, providing regular check-ups, and referring patients to specialists when needed.

Another important aspect of a GP's job is to provide emotional support and counseling to their patients. Many people seek medical care not only for physical ailments, but also for mental health issues. GPs are trained to provide support and guidance to patients who are dealing with emotional or psychological challenges.

In addition to providing medical care, GPs are also responsible for managing the administrative aspects of their practice. This includes keeping accurate medical records, billing patients and insurance companies, and managing staff and resources.

Overall, being a GP is a challenging and rewarding profession. GPs have the opportunity to make a real difference in the lives of their patients and help keep their communities healthy. If you are interested in becoming a GP, you will need to be dedicated, compassionate, and committed to providing high-quality medical care to your patients.

GEOLOGIST

Geologists are scientists who study the Earth, its composition, and the processes that shape and change it over time. They use their knowledge of geology to explore the planet, understand its history, and discover resources like minerals, oil, and natural gas. They play a crucial role in helping us understand how the Earth works and how we can best use its resources in a sustainable way.

One of the primary tasks of geologists is to study rocks and minerals. They examine samples of these materials to determine their composition and properties, such as density, color, and texture. Geologists also use specialized tools and techniques to study the geological features of the Earth's surface, such as mountains, valleys, and canyons.

Geologists use their understanding of the physical processes that shape the Earth, such as plate tectonics and erosion, to identify potential geological hazards, such as earthquakes, landslides, and volcanic eruptions. They work to predict the likelihood and severity of these events, as well as their potential impact on people and the environment. By doing so, they help to reduce the risk of damage and loss of life from natural disasters.

Another important area of work for geologists is resource exploration. They use their knowledge of the Earth's composition to locate valuable minerals and natural resources. This includes oil and natural gas, which are used to power our homes and vehicles, as well as precious metals like gold and silver that are used in jewelry and electronics.

Geologists also play a key role in environmental protection and conservation efforts. By studying the Earth's natural systems and how they interact with human activity, they can identify ways to mitigate negative environmental impacts and promote sustainable practices. They help to protect water sources, wildlife habitats, and natural areas by monitoring and assessing the effects of human activities on the environment.

They must be able to analyze complex data sets and communicate their findings clearly and effectively. Geologists often work in teams and collaborate with other scientists, engineers, and professionals to achieve their goals.

If you're interested in becoming a geologist you'll need a solid foundation in science and math, as well as a degree in geology or a related field.

GLASSBLOWER

Have you ever seen a beautiful glass vase or a unique glass sculpture and wondered how it was made? Well, one profession that is responsible for creating these pieces of art is that of a glassblower. Glassblowers are skilled craftsmen who work with molten glass to create a wide range of objects, from delicate ornaments to large architectural installations.

At its core, glassblowing is the art of shaping and manipulating molten glass using specialized tools and techniques. The process involves heating glass to a high temperature until it becomes soft and pliable, then working with it using a variety of tools to shape it into the desired form.

The first step in the glassblowing process is to gather molten glass on the end of a long, hollow tube called a blowpipe. The glassblower then shapes the molten glass by rolling, pulling, and blowing it into the desired shape, using tools such as paddles, tweezers, and shears to manipulate the glass.

Glassblowers must have a strong understanding of the properties of glass, including its melting point, elasticity, and how it reacts to temperature changes. They must also have a good eye for detail and be skilled at working quickly and accurately, as the glass cools and hardens rapidly.

In addition to creating unique and beautiful glass objects, glassblowers may also repair damaged glassware or create custom pieces based on a customer's specifications. They may work in a variety of settings, including glassblowing studios, factories, and even museums.

One of the most famous examples of glassblowing is the art of Venetian glassblowing, which has been practiced for centuries in Venice, Italy. Venetian glassblowers are known for their intricate and colorful glass objects, such as chandeliers, vases, and figurines.

Glassblowing can be a physically demanding profession, as it requires standing for long periods of time and working with heavy equipment. However, for those with a passion for the art, it can be an incredibly rewarding and fulfilling career.

In addition to creating unique and beautiful glass objects, glassblowers may also teach their craft to others, passing on their knowledge and skills to future generations of glassblowers.

So, if you're fascinated by the beauty and intricacy of glass art, and have a passion for working with your hands, glassblowing might just be the perfect profession for you!

GRAPHIC DESIGNER

A graphic designer is a creative professional who combines artistic talent and technical expertise to communicate ideas through visual elements. They create designs for various media, such as websites, logos, brochures, advertisements, and product packaging. A career in graphic design offers a unique opportunity to blend creativity, problem-solving skills, and a keen eye for aesthetics, making it an exciting choice for those with a passion for visual storytelling.

To become a graphic designer, one typically needs a foundation in design principles, software, and techniques. Many professionals hold a degree in graphic design or a related field, such as illustration or fine arts. However, others may acquire their skills through self-study, online courses, or workshops. Building a diverse and impressive portfolio of projects is essential for showcasing skills and attracting potential employers or clients.

Graphic designers work with clients or creative teams to understand their design needs and develop visual solutions that effectively convey their message. They create drafts or mock-ups, refine their ideas based on feedback, and produce final designs that meet the project's goals. In addition, they must stay current with design trends and software updates, continuously honing their skills and adapting to the ever-evolving industry.

An engaging example of a graphic designer's work might involve designing a logo and packaging for a new organic snack brand. The designer would need to capture the brand's essence and convey its commitment to sustainability and healthy eating through the choice of colors, typography, and imagery. A well-crafted design could help the brand stand out on store shelves and resonate with its target audience, contributing to the product's success in the market.

Graphic designers may specialize in specific areas, such as branding, digital design, or print media, depending on their interests and expertise. The role often involves a flexible schedule, allowing graphic designers to balance multiple projects and meet deadlines as needed.

The demand for skilled graphic designers is expected to grow, driven by the need for visually compelling content across digital and traditional media. As technology continues to advance, new opportunities may emerge for graphic designers to create innovative and immersive experiences, such as virtual reality or augmented reality environments.

HAIR STYLIST

Hairstylists, also known as hairdressers, are professionals who specialize in cutting, styling, coloring, and treating hair. They work in hair salons, spas, and other establishments that offer hair and beauty services.

Hairstylists are artists who use hair as their medium to create works of art. They are skilled in a wide range of techniques, from classic haircuts to more creative and avant-garde styles. A good hairstylist knows how to bring out the best in each client, taking into consideration their face shape, hair type, and personal style.

Hairstylists typically start by consulting with the client to determine their needs and preferences. They may ask about the client's lifestyle, hair type, face shape, and other factors that can impact the style. Based on this information, the hairstylist will recommend a hairstyle that will flatter the client's features and suit their lifestyle.

Once the client has agreed on the hairstyle, the hairstylist will get to work. They may start by washing and conditioning the hair to prepare it for cutting or styling. They will use a variety of tools, including scissors, razors, combs, and brushes, to create the desired look.

Hairstylists also specialize in hair coloring, which involves changing the natural color of the hair. They use a range of products, from temporary hair dyes to permanent color, to achieve the desired shade. They may also use highlighting or lowlighting techniques to add depth to the hair.

In addition to cutting and styling hair, hairstylists are also trained in hair treatments such as conditioning, perming, and straightening. These treatments can help to improve the texture and health of the hair, making it more manageable and shiny.

Hairstylists must also stay up-to-date with the latest trends and techniques in the industry. They may attend training and education sessions to learn new skills and keep their skills sharp. They may also be required to work with a wide range of hair types and textures, from fine and straight to thick and curly.

One of the most important skills for a hairstylist is communication. They must be able to communicate effectively with their clients to understand their needs and preferences. They must also be able to give clear instructions and provide feedback to their clients on how to maintain their hair between salon visits.

Hairstylists may work in a range of settings, from small independent salons to large chain establishments. They may also work in spas, hotels, and other businesses that offer hair and beauty services.

HISTORIAN

Historians are people who study history. History is the study of the past, and historians use a variety of sources to learn about what happened in the past. They might read old books, look at pictures and artifacts, or interview people who were alive during the time period they are studying.

One of the most important things that historians do is try to understand why things happened the way they did in the past. For example, they might study why certain wars were fought or why people lived the way they did in a particular time and place. By understanding the past, historians hope to learn from it and to make better decisions in the present and future.

There are many different types of historians. Some historians specialize in a particular time period or place, while others focus on a particular topic or theme. For example, a historian might study the history of the United States during the Civil War, or the history of ancient Greece.

Historians also use a variety of tools and techniques to study the past. They might analyze old documents to try to understand the language and context in which they were written. They might use statistics and other data to try to understand trends and patterns in history, and also computers and digital databases to organize and analyze their data.

One of the most important skills that historians have is the ability to ask good questions. By asking questions, historians can try to uncover new information and gain new insights into the past. They might also try to challenge existing beliefs and ideas about history, in order to better understand what actually happened in the past.

Historians also play an important role in society. They help us to understand where we came from and how we got to where we are today. They also help us to appreciate the complexity of human history, and to better understand our place in the world.

If you are interested in becoming a historian, there are many different career paths you can take. You might become a professor and teach history at a university, or work for a museum or historical society. You might also work in government or the private sector.

In summary, historians are people who study history and try to understand why things happened the way they did in the past. They use a variety of sources and techniques to uncover new information and gain new insights into the past. Historians play an important role in helping us understand where we came from and how we got to where we are today.

HUMAN RESOURCES MANAGER

A human resources manager is a professional responsible for recruiting, training, and managing a company's employees. They are the backbone of any organization and are in charge of ensuring that employees are happy, motivated, and working towards a common goal.

A human resources manager wears many hats and has a wide range of responsibilities. They are in charge of recruitment and hiring, as well as developing and implementing training programs to help employees perform their jobs effectively. They are also responsible for managing employee benefits, overseeing performance evaluations, and handling any employee complaints or concerns.

One of the most exciting parts of being a human resources manager is that they get to work with people from all backgrounds and with all kinds of skills. They are the ones who identify talent and bring people on board to help the company grow. They work with employees at every level, from entry-level positions to executive management, and ensure that each person is given the support they need to succeed.

Another exciting part of being a human resources manager is that they get to help shape the culture of the organization. They work with leadership to create policies and procedures that align with the company's values and goals, and they are responsible for ensuring that employees feel comfortable and engaged in the workplace. They work to create a positive and inclusive work environment where all employees feel valued and supported.

Human resources managers are also responsible for ensuring that the company is compliant with all relevant laws and regulations. They stay up-to-date on changes to labor laws and make sure that the company is adhering to them. This includes things like ensuring that employees are paid fairly, that they have access to the benefits they are entitled to, and that the company is following all safety guidelines.

In addition to all of these responsibilities, human resources managers are often called upon to handle difficult situations and make tough decisions. For example, they may need to mediate disputes between employees, address issues of workplace harassment, or make difficult decisions about terminating employees.

Overall, being a human resources manager is a career that requires the ability to work well with people, understand the needs of the organization, and navigate complex legal and regulatory environments.

INDUSTRIAL ENGINEER

An industrial engineer is a professional who focuses on improving the efficiency and effectiveness of various production processes. They use their skills to ensure that products are made in the most cost-effective, efficient, and safe way possible.

Imagine you work in a factory that produces bicycles. An industrial engineer would be the one who makes sure that the bicycles are made in the most efficient way possible. They would look at the entire process from beginning to end, including the steps for assembling the bikes, painting them, packaging them, and shipping them to the stores. They would then use their knowledge of engineering and production to find ways to streamline the process, making it faster, cheaper, and safer.

For example, an industrial engineer might suggest that the bikes be painted using a different method that is faster and produces less waste. They might also suggest changes to the assembly process to reduce the amount of time it takes to build each bike, or to improve the quality of the finished product. They may also analyze data to identify bottlenecks in the production process and develop strategies to address them.

Industrial engineers are also responsible for ensuring that the workers are safe while on the job. They may develop safety protocols, train employees, and identify potential hazards in the workplace. They will also work with management to make sure that the company is in compliance with all relevant safety regulations.

In addition to working in manufacturing, industrial engineers can also be found in a variety of other industries. They may work in healthcare, helping hospitals and clinics improve their processes and patient care. They may also work in logistics, optimizing supply chain and transportation processes. They can also be found in consulting firms, where they advise companies on how to improve their overall operations and efficiency.

If you're interested in becoming an industrial engineer, you should have a strong background in math, science, and engineering. You'll need to be able to analyze data, identify problems, and come up with innovative solutions. You'll also need to have strong communication skills, as you'll be working with a variety of people across different departments.

Industrial engineering is an exciting and dynamic field that offers a lot of opportunities for growth and advancement. As technology continues to evolve, the demand for skilled industrial engineers will only continue to increase.

INSURANCE AGENT

Have you ever wondered what happens when your house is damaged in a storm, or your car gets into an accident, or you or someone in your family gets sick or injured and needs medical treatment? These kinds of unexpected events can be scary and stressful, but that's where insurance comes in. Insurance is a type of protection that people can buy to help them pay for the costs of unexpected events that might happen in the future. And that's where insurance agents come in - they help people choose the right insurance policies to protect themselves and their families.

So, what exactly does an insurance agent do? Well, first of all, they work for insurance companies. Insurance companies create the policies that people can buy to protect themselves, and insurance agents are the ones who sell those policies to customers. Insurance agents might work for large national insurance companies, or they might work for smaller local insurance agencies. But no matter where they work, their job is to help people figure out what kind of insurance they need and then sell them a policy.

One of the most important parts of an insurance agent's job is helping people choose the right insurance policies. There are many different types of insurance policies, each designed to protect people from different kinds of risks. For example, there are car insurance policies that protect drivers in case they get into a car accident, home insurance policies that protect homeowners in case their houses are damaged, and health insurance policies that help people pay for medical treatment.

But insurance agents don't just sell insurance policies and then walk away. They also help their clients when something goes wrong and they need to make a claim on their policy. Making a claim means asking the insurance company to pay for something that's covered by the policy, like a car repair or a medical bill. Insurance agents help their clients fill out the necessary paperwork and make sure they get the money they're entitled to.

Additionally, insurance agents also work with businesses to help them get protected from unexpected risks. Businesses need insurance policies just like people do, but the types of policies they need can be more complex. For example, a small business might need liability insurance to protect them if someone gets hurt on their property, or business interruption insurance to help them pay their bills if they have to shut down temporarily.

Insurance agents need to be good communicators, good listeners, and good problem-solvers. They need to be able to explain complex insurance policies in simple terms, listen carefully to their clients' needs and concerns, and come up with creative solutions to help them get the coverage they need.

INTERIOR DESIGNER

Interior designers are professionals who create functional and aesthetically pleasing interior spaces. They work with clients to design spaces that meet their needs and preferences while also ensuring that the space is safe, comfortable, and visually appealing.

Interior designers are responsible for creating and implementing design plans that meet the needs of their clients. They work on a wide range of spaces, including residential homes, commercial buildings, and public spaces. They may work on everything from individual rooms to entire buildings, and their goal is to create spaces that are both beautiful and functional.

One of the key responsibilities of an interior designer is to create a design plan for a space. This involves meeting with clients to discuss their needs, preferences, and budget, as well as taking measurements of the space and creating sketches and renderings of potential designs. Once the design plan is finalized, the interior designer will work to source materials, furnishings, and décor that fit within the design scheme.

Interior designers may work on a variety of different projects, from designing custom furniture and cabinetry to choosing the perfect paint color for a room. They also work with contractors and other professionals to oversee the construction or renovation of a space. This may involve working with architects, electricians, plumbers, and other professionals to ensure that the space is designed and built to code and meets the needs of the client.

In addition to designing spaces, interior designers are also responsible for staying up-to-date on the latest trends and technologies in the industry. This may involve attending trade shows and conferences, keeping up with design blogs and magazines, and taking continuing education courses to stay current on best practices and new techniques.

Interior designers also need to be skilled at communicating and working with clients. They need to be able to listen to their clients' needs and preferences, communicate their design plans clearly, and be able to adapt their plans based on feedback from their clients. They also need to be able to manage budgets, timelines, and contractors to ensure that projects are completed on time and within budget.

If you're interested in becoming an interior designer, you'll typically need a bachelor's degree in interior design or a related field, and you may also need to complete an internship or apprenticeship to gain practical experience. You'll also need strong design skills, an eye for detail, and excellent communication and problem-solving skills.

INVESTMENT BANKER

An investment banker is a professional who works with companies and governments to help them raise money by issuing and selling stocks, bonds, and other financial products to investors. Investment bankers help clients evaluate the risks and benefits of different financial strategies and help them make decisions about how to raise capital in the most effective way.

To become an investment banker, you need a strong educational background in finance and economics. Investment bankers usually hold a bachelor's degree in business or finance, and many go on to earn a Master of Business Administration (MBA) degree.

One of the main roles of an investment banker is to help companies raise capital. This can involve evaluating the financial health of the company and advising on the best way to structure a deal. Investment bankers may help clients raise funds through a variety of methods, including public offerings, private placements, and debt financing.

Another key responsibility of an investment banker is to help clients manage their financial risk. This can include helping them hedge against fluctuations in currency or interest rates, or advising them on how to invest their money in the most effective way. Investment bankers may also work with clients to create financial models that can help them understand how different scenarios might play out over time.

Investment bankers often work in large financial institutions, such as investment banks, commercial banks, or hedge funds. They may work in a variety of roles, including corporate finance, mergers and acquisitions, and sales and trading.

One of the most exciting aspects of working as an investment banker is the opportunity to work on high-profile deals. Investment bankers may work with clients in a variety of industries, including technology, healthcare, energy, and finance. They may help companies go public, acquire other companies, or raise funds to finance new projects.

Investment banking can also be a highly lucrative career. Investment bankers typically earn a base salary and typically receive bonuses that can be worth several times their base salary.

However, investment banking is also a demanding and high-pressure profession. Investment bankers often work long hours and must be able to juggle multiple projects and clients simultaneously. They must also be able to work well under pressure and be comfortable making quick decisions in fast-paced environments.

IT SPECIALIST

An IT (Information Technology) specialist is a skilled professional who manages, maintains, and troubleshoots technology systems within an organization. They play a critical role in ensuring that businesses and institutions can operate smoothly, securely, and efficiently in a digital world. A career as an IT specialist offers a diverse range of opportunities for individuals with a passion for technology, problem-solving, and helping others.

To become an IT specialist, one typically needs a strong foundation in computer science, information systems, or a related field. Many professionals hold a bachelor's degree, while others may pursue certifications or technical training through vocational schools, or community colleges. Gaining hands-on experience, such as internships or entry-level positions, is essential for developing the practical skills required in the IT field.

IT specialists work with various technologies, including computer hardware, software, networks, and databases. Their responsibilities can vary depending on their specific role, but may include installing and configuring systems, diagnosing and resolving technical issues, ensuring data security, and providing user support.

A normal day for an IT specialist might involve implementing a new network infrastructure for a small business. The specialist would assess the company's needs, design a secure and scalable network architecture, and install the necessary hardware and software components. By setting up a reliable and efficient network, the IT specialist would enable the business to connect employees, share resources, and access the internet seamlessly, ultimately contributing to the company's growth and success.

IT specialists can find employment in various industries, as most organizations rely on technology to function effectively. Some IT specialists choose to specialize in specific areas, such as cybersecurity, cloud computing, or database administration, depending on their interests and expertise.

In conclusion, a career as an IT specialist offers a unique blend of technical knowledge, problem-solving skills, and the chance to make a meaningful impact on the way organizations operate in a digital world. IT specialists play an essential role in ensuring the reliability, security, and efficiency of technology systems, enabling businesses and institutions to thrive and adapt to an ever-changing technological landscape.

JEWELER

Jewelers are people who make, repair, and sell jewelry. Jewelry can be made from a variety of materials such as precious metals, gems, and other materials. A jeweler's job is to create beautiful pieces of jewelry that can be worn and appreciated by people all around the world.

Jewelers need to be skilled in working with precious metals and gems. They use a range of tools and techniques to create intricate designs that are unique and beautiful. They may use a variety of materials such as gold, silver, platinum, diamonds, and other precious stones to create their pieces. Some jewelers specialize in a particular type of jewelry, such as wedding rings, necklaces, or bracelets.

Jewelers may start with a design sketch, which is then turned into a 3D model using computer-aided design (CAD) software. Once the design is finalized, the jeweler begins the process of creating the piece. This may involve using a range of tools, including hammers, pliers, and cutters, to shape and form the metal into the desired shape. Stones are then carefully set into the metal to create the finished piece.

Repairing jewelry is also an important part of a jeweler's job. Jewelry can become damaged over time or through wear and tear, and a jeweler can repair these pieces to their original condition. This may involve repairing or replacing broken clasps, resetting stones, or polishing the metal to restore its shine.

Jewelers also work in retail settings, where they sell jewelry to customers. In these settings, they may interact with customers to help them find the perfect piece of jewelry for a special occasion, such as a wedding or anniversary.

In addition to making and selling jewelry, jewelers must also stay up to date with the latest trends and styles. They attend trade shows and keep an eye on fashion trends to ensure that their jewelry remains relevant and desirable to their customers.

Jewelers may work in a variety of settings, from small independent workshops to large jewelry manufacturing companies. Some may specialize in a particular type of jewelry, while others may create custom pieces for clients.

To become a jeweler, you will need to have a combination of artistic talent and technical skill. You may start by completing an apprenticeship with a master jeweler, or you may choose to pursue a degree in jewelry design. In addition to these skills, a successful jeweler must have excellent attention to detail, patience, and the ability to work with precision and accuracy.

JOURNALIST

Journalists are the eyes and ears of the world. They have a unique power to shape public opinion, influence policy decisions, and keep people informed about what is happening in the world around them. A journalist's job is to gather, analyze, and report on news and events to the public, and they work in a wide range of media, including newspapers, magazines, TV news programs, and online media.

Journalists are the people who keep us informed about the world, and they do so by uncovering stories and investigating issues that are important to the public. They identify, research, and report on news stories, whether they are local, national, or international. Journalists work to deliver accurate and unbiased information, and they strive to provide a clear and comprehensive picture of the world around us.

One of the most important roles of a journalist is to gather information. This involves researching, interviewing, and investigating to get the facts and details of a story. They often attend press conferences, meetings, and events to gather information and quotes from the sources. They may also rely on tips and leads from the public, whistleblowers, or other sources to uncover stories.

Once the information has been gathered, journalists must then analyze it and determine its relevance and importance to the public. This involves checking the facts, verifying the sources, and understanding the context and implications of the story. Journalists use critical thinking skills to identify patterns, and trends in the information they gather.

With this information, journalists then write articles, reports, or produce segments for their medium of choice. They craft compelling stories that inform and engage their audiences, using language that is clear and accessible to the general public.

Journalists are also responsible for protecting their sources and maintaining their confidentiality. They must also work within the boundaries of journalistic ethics, which include avoiding conflicts of interest, and striving for accuracy in their reporting.

Journalists must also be able to work under pressure and tight deadlines. Breaking news stories can happen at any time, and journalists must be able to quickly gather and report on them. They may also be required to work long hours and to travel to different locations to cover stories.

JUDGE

A judge is a person who presides over a court of law, hearing legal cases and making decisions based on the facts and evidence presented in court. Judges are the guardians of the law and ensure it is followed and that justice is served in a fair and impartial manner.

Judges have a wide range of responsibilities, but some of their most important duties include the following:

1. Presiding over Legal Proceedings: This can include criminal trials, civil cases, and family law cases, among others. During these proceedings, the judge ensures that both sides are following the rules of evidence and procedure, and that everyone is given a fair chance to present their case.

2. Interpreting the Law: Judges are responsible for interpreting and applying the law to the cases that come before them. They must have a thorough understanding of the law and be able to apply it to specific situations in a fair and impartial manner.

3. Making Decisions: Judges are responsible for making decisions in legal cases. This can include deciding which evidence is admissible, ruling on objections made by lawyers, and determining guilt or innocence in criminal cases. In civil cases, judges may have to decide how much money a plaintiff is entitled to receive, or which party is responsible for a particular problem.

4. Writing Opinions: After making a decision, judges must write an opinion that explains their reasoning. These detailed opinions provide guidance to other judges in similar cases.

5. Conducting Hearings: In addition to trials, judges may also conduct hearings on various legal issues, such as whether to grant bail to a defendant or to determine child custody in a divorce case.

The role of a judge is crucial to our legal system. They play a vital role in maintaining order and stability in our society, by upholding the law and protecting individual rights. Without judges, our legal system would be chaotic and unpredictable, and people would not be able to rely on a fair and impartial system for resolving disputes.

Becoming a judge requires a great deal of education and experience. Typically, a person must first earn a law degree, then work as an attorney for several years before being considered for a judgeship. Some judges are appointed by elected officials, while others are elected by the people. Regardless of how they are chosen, judges must be highly knowledgeable about the law and have a strong sense of integrity and impartiality.

LANDSCAPER

A landscaper is a professional who designs, creates, and maintains outdoor spaces. They work to create and maintain a range of outdoor spaces, from small residential gardens to large public parks. Landscaping is a multi-disciplinary profession that involves elements of design, horticulture, and construction. As such, a skilled landscaper must be knowledgeable in a wide range of areas, including botany, engineering, design, and environmental science.

The primary goal of a landscaper is to create a visually appealing and functional outdoor space. They work with clients to understand their needs and preferences, and then develop a plan that meets those requirements while also taking into account the local environment and climate. This may include designing and installing various features, such as gardens, water features, walkways, patios, and lighting.

In addition to designing and installing these features, a landscaper is also responsible for maintaining them. This may include regular maintenance such as mowing lawns, pruning plants, and fertilizing soil, as well as more extensive maintenance such as repairing or replacing damaged features.

Landscapers work in a variety of settings, including residential properties, commercial buildings, parks, golf courses, and other public spaces. Some landscapers work for large landscaping companies, while others are self-employed.

One of the most important skills for a landscaper is the ability to design and plan outdoor spaces. This requires a deep understanding of plant biology, hardscaping materials, and construction techniques. Landscapers must be able to create detailed plans that include information about plant placement, materials, and costs.

In addition to design skills, a landscaper must also possess a strong understanding of the environment and local ecology. This includes knowledge of the local climate, soil composition, and native plant species. A skilled landscaper can work with these factors to create a sustainable outdoor space that is both beautiful and functional.

Another important aspect of a landscaper's job is project management. They must be able coordinate the various aspects of a landscaping project, including designing, planning, purchasing materials, and coordinating the work of other contractors.

Landscaping can be a physically demanding job, as it often involves manual labor such as lifting heavy materials and using power tools. As a result, a landscaper must be in good physical condition and have the ability to work outdoors in changing weather conditions.

LAWYER

A lawyer is someone who practices law, which is a system of rules that governs society and regulates behavior. Lawyers help people navigate this complex system by giving them legal advice and representing them in court.

Lawyers can work in a variety of different areas, such as criminal law, civil law, family law, corporate law, environmental law, and more. They can also work in different settings, such as law firms, government agencies, corporations, and non-profit organizations.

One of the most important jobs of a lawyer is to provide legal advice to their clients. This involves helping their clients understand their legal rights and responsibilities, as well as the potential consequences of their actions. Lawyers also help their clients navigate the legal system by explaining the different procedures and steps involved in a legal case.

In addition to providing legal advice, lawyers also represent their clients in court. This involves preparing legal documents, such as briefs and pleadings, and presenting arguments in front of a judge or jury. Lawyers also cross-examine witnesses and question expert witnesses in order to present the best possible case for their client.

Lawyers also play an important role in negotiating settlements between parties. This involves working with the opposing side to find a mutually acceptable resolution to a legal dispute. Lawyers use their knowledge of the law and their negotiation skills to help their clients reach a fair and just settlement.

Another important job of a lawyer is to keep up with changes in the law. Laws are constantly changing and evolving, and it is the job of the lawyer to stay up-to-date on these changes in order to provide the best possible legal advice to their clients.

To become a lawyer, you typically need to obtain a law degree and pass the bar exam in the state in which you want to practice. Law school is a rigorous three-year program that involves studying many different areas of the law, such as contracts, torts, property, and criminal law. After graduating from law school, aspiring lawyers must pass the bar exam, which tests their knowledge of the law and their ability to apply it in real-world situations.

Lawyers can help people navigate a complex legal system and to advocate for their clients' rights. Whether you're interested in criminal law, environmental law, or corporate law, becoming a lawyer is a great way to make a difference in the world and to help people in need.

LIBRARIAN

A librarian is a professional who helps people access information and navigate the vast world of books and other materials. They can work in different types of libraries such as public libraries, school libraries, academic libraries, and specialized libraries, such as medical or law libraries.

The librarian's main responsibility is to help library users find the information they need. They often work at a reference desk, where they answer questions, assist with research projects, and recommend materials based on the user's interests and needs. They also organize and maintain library collections, including books, periodicals, audiovisual materials, and electronic resources.

Librarians also create programs and activities for library patrons. They might organize reading clubs, book fairs, or author visits. They also plan and host special events, such as workshops, story hours for children, and job search assistance.

In addition to helping patrons access information, librarians are also responsible for organizing and maintaining the library's collection. This involves choosing which materials to acquire and making sure that the materials are properly cataloged and shelved. They are also responsible for evaluating the library's collection to ensure that it meets the needs of the community it serves. For example, if the library is located in a community with a high Spanish-speaking population, the librarian might choose to acquire more Spanish-language materials to meet the community's needs.

Librarians also play an important role in helping people develop research skills. They teach people how to find and evaluate information, which is an essential skill in today's information age. This includes showing people how to use library resources, such as databases and search engines, as well as other research tools.

In addition to working with the public, librarians also work with other professionals, such as teachers, researchers, and other librarians. They might collaborate with teachers to develop lesson plans or work with researchers to provide access to specialized resources.

One important aspect of a librarian's job is staying up-to-date with the latest technology and trends. Many libraries now offer e-books, audiobooks, and other digital resources, and librarians must be able to navigate and troubleshoot these digital platforms.

Becoming a librarian requires a master's degree in library science. Librarians also need strong interpersonal skills and a love for books and information. Additionally, they must be comfortable working with people of all ages and backgrounds.

LOAN OFFICER

Aspiring homeowners, car buyers, and small business owners rely on loans to finance their purchases. A loan officer is a financial expert who helps individuals and organizations secure financing from banks and other financial institutions. The role of a loan officer is to assess a client's creditworthiness, risk, and financial stability to determine their eligibility for a loan.

Loan officers play a critical role in the lending process. They help clients navigate the often-complex application process, negotiate loan terms, and provide expert advice to ensure that clients are getting the best deal possible. As a result, loan officers must possess a strong understanding of banking regulations, credit analysis, and lending practices.

A loan officer's day-to-day responsibilities may include reviewing loan applications, assessing clients' creditworthiness, and analyzing financial documents such as tax returns, bank statements, and credit reports. Once a loan application is approved, the loan officer will work with the client to determine the best loan product and interest rate based on the client's needs and financial situation.

Loan officers must have excellent communication skills to explain the often-complicated lending process to clients in a way that they can understand. They must be able to build relationships with clients and have a thorough understanding of lending regulations, interest rates, and loan products to provide clients with the best advice.

Successful loan officers must be able to work under pressure, meet strict deadlines, and be comfortable working with numbers and data. They must also have strong analytical skills and be able to quickly assess a client's financial health to determine whether they are eligible for a loan.

Loan officers work in a variety of settings, including banks, credit unions, mortgage companies, and other financial institutions. They may work in a branch office or remotely, using technology to communicate with clients and assess loan applications.

While a college degree is not always required to become a loan officer, most financial institutions prefer candidates with a degree in finance, accounting, or a related field. Additionally, loan officers must complete a training program to gain the necessary knowledge and skills to work in the field.

Loan officers also play a vital role in times of economic uncertainty. During the 2008 financial crisis, experienced loan officers were instrumental in helping homeowners navigate refinancing options and avoid foreclosure. They served as financial lifeguards, keeping families afloat during tumultuous times.

LOGISTICIAN

A logistician is a professional who is responsible for managing and coordinating the movement of goods and materials from one location to another. This involves planning, organizing, and directing the supply chain and ensuring that everything runs smoothly.

Logisticians work in a variety of industries, including manufacturing, retail, transportation, and the military. They are responsible for managing everything from raw materials to finished products and ensuring that they get to their destination on time and in good condition.

One of the key responsibilities of a logistician is to analyze and evaluate the supply chain. They need to understand the entire process from start to finish, from the sourcing of raw materials to the delivery of the finished product. They use this knowledge to identify areas where the supply chain can be improved, such as reducing transportation costs, improving inventory management, and optimizing production schedules.

Another important aspect of a logistician's job is to coordinate with various stakeholders in the supply chain. This includes working with suppliers to ensure that they are delivering goods on time and at the right quality, as well as working with transportation companies to schedule and track shipments. They also work closely with production managers to ensure that materials are available when needed, and with sales teams to forecast demand and adjust production schedules accordingly.

Logisticians also use a variety of software tools to help them manage the supply chain. These tools include inventory management systems, transportation management systems, and enterprise resource planning (ERP) software. They use these tools to track inventory levels, monitor shipments, and identify potential bottlenecks in the supply chain.

Another important aspect of a logistician's job is to ensure that all shipments comply with local, state, and federal regulations. This can be a complex task, as different countries and regions have different rules and regulations regarding the transport of goods. Logisticians need to be familiar with these regulations and ensure that all shipments are in compliance.

Finally, logisticians are responsible for managing the budget for the supply chain. They need to ensure that all costs are accounted for, including the cost of raw materials, transportation, and labor. They also need to identify ways to reduce costs and improve efficiency, such as consolidating shipments or negotiating better rates with transportation providers.

MACHINE LEARNING ENGINEER

A machine learning engineer is a computer science professional who specializes in developing artificial intelligence (AI) algorithms and systems that enable machines to learn and make decisions without being explicitly programmed. They work with large amounts of data to train machine learning models, fine-tune algorithms, and develop software that can be used in a variety of applications.

As machine learning algorithms become increasingly important in industry, government, and academia, the role of the machine learning engineer has become more critical. The ability to build and improve intelligent systems that can learn from data is a key driver of innovation in a wide range of industries, including healthcare, finance, transportation, and more.

Machine learning engineers are responsible for designing and developing machine learning systems that can learn from data and make predictions. They work with large amounts of data to create models and algorithms that can recognize patterns and make accurate predictions. Machine learning engineers must also have a solid understanding of computer science, mathematics, and statistics to develop models that are both accurate and efficient.

To develop machine learning systems, machine learning engineers must first understand the problem they are trying to solve. They work closely with data scientists and domain experts to identify the key features and patterns in the data. They then use this information to develop machine learning models that can recognize and predict patterns in new data.

Once a model has been developed, machine learning engineers must fine-tune it to improve its accuracy and efficiency. They may use techniques like cross-validation, regularization, and feature selection to improve the performance of the model. They must also work to ensure that the model is scalable and can handle large volumes of data.

In addition to designing and developing machine learning systems, machine learning engineers must also ensure that they are deployed and integrated correctly. They may work with software engineers and IT professionals to deploy models in production environments, and they may develop APIs and other interfaces to allow other applications to interact with the machine learning system.

Machine learning engineers must also stay up-to-date with the latest developments in the field of AI and machine learning. They must be able to evaluate new techniques and tools and determine whether they can be used to improve the performance of their models.

MACHINIST

Machinists are skilled tradespeople who use machine tools and precision instruments to produce precision metal parts, components, and tools. They set up and operate various types of machines, such as lathes, milling machines, grinders, and drill presses, to produce a wide range of products that are used in various industries.

Machinists work with a wide variety of metals and plastics, including steel, aluminum, titanium, and brass, to name a few. They work from blueprints, drawings, and specifications to plan and produce parts that meet precise tolerances and specifications. This requires the ability to read and interpret technical documents, understand complex geometric and mathematical concepts, and use computer-aided design (CAD) software to create and modify digital designs.

One of the most important tasks of a machinist is to set up and operate machine tools to cut, drill, shape, and finish metal parts. They use a variety of cutting tools, such as drills, lathes, and milling machines, to create precise cuts and shapes. They also use precision instruments, such as micrometers, gauges, and calipers, to measure and test the parts they produce to ensure that they meet the required specifications.

Machinists must be able to work with a variety of materials, including metals and plastics, and must have knowledge of the properties of different materials and how they can be shaped and formed. They must also be able to use different cutting tools and techniques to achieve the desired results.

Machinists may work in a variety of industries, including automotive, aerospace, and manufacturing. They may work in machine shops, factories, or other industrial settings.

They must be able to work effectively in a team environment, and they must be able to communicate with engineers and designers to ensure that they understand the requirements of each project.

Machinists are also responsible for maintaining and repairing the machines they use. This involves regular cleaning, lubrication, and maintenance of the machines to ensure that they are in good working order. They must also be able to diagnose and repair problems with the machines, such as mechanical or electrical problems.

To become a machinist, one typically needs a high school diploma or equivalent, and may also need to complete a vocational training program or an apprenticeship. This training can take several years, and typically includes a combination of classroom instruction and on-the-job training.

MAKEUP ARTIST

Makeup artists are professionals who apply makeup and other cosmetic products to enhance the appearance of their clients. These professionals work in various settings such as beauty salons, television and film sets, theatrical productions, and special events such as weddings and fashion shows. They are responsible for selecting and applying makeup products that complement their client's skin tone, facial features, and desired look.

One of the primary roles of a makeup artist is to enhance the natural beauty of their clients. This means that they must have a keen eye for detail and be able to identify the features of their client's face that require accentuation. They must be able to choose the right products that suit their client's skin type and tone, and be knowledgeable about different cosmetic brands and products that are available in the market.

In addition to enhancing the natural features of their clients, makeup artists are also responsible for creating dramatic or specialized looks. These may include special effects makeup for theatrical productions, movie and TV sets, and special events such as Halloween parties. They must have a good understanding of different makeup techniques and be able to use various tools to create different effects.

Makeup artists are also responsible for maintaining their clients' makeup throughout the day or the duration of the event. This means they must be knowledgeable about the different types of cosmetic products, and be able to apply them in a way that ensures they remain in place for extended periods. They must also be able to make touch-ups and adjustments as needed, and ensure that their clients are comfortable and satisfied.

A key responsibility of a makeup artist is to maintain a high level of hygiene and sanitation in their work environment. They must regularly clean their tools, brushes, and workstations to ensure that they are free from bacteria and other harmful microorganisms. They must also be able to maintain a clean and organized work area that is conducive to creativity and productivity.

Makeup artists must also have excellent communication skills. They must be able to communicate effectively with their clients, understand their preferences and expectations, and make recommendations on the best products and techniques that will help them achieve their desired look. They must also be able to work well under pressure and have a professional demeanor that puts their clients at ease.

MARINE BIOLOGIST

A marine biologist's career path is an enthralling journey of scientific discovery, where curious minds delve into the mysterious world beneath the waves. Imagine spending your days exploring vibrant coral reefs, observing the balletic dance of dolphins, or researching the enigmatic lives of deep-sea creatures. As a marine biologist, you will not only be a custodian of marine life but also an ambassador for its conservation.

Embarking on this captivating career path starts with a solid foundation in the sciences. Aspiring marine biologists should consider pursuing a Bachelor's degree in marine biology, biology, or a related field. During your undergraduate studies, you'll be immersed in courses like oceanography, marine ecology, and genetics, which will equip you with the knowledge and skills to unlock the secrets of the marine world. This is also the perfect time to gain practical experience by volunteering or interning at research centers, aquaria, or marine conservation organizations.

Next, you'll want to pursue a Master's or Doctorate degree to specialize in your area of interest within marine biology. You could choose to focus on the intricacies of coral reef ecosystems, the enigmatic behavior of sharks, or the complex network of marine food webs. Graduate programs offer hands-on research opportunities, allowing you to work closely with faculty members and dive deeper into your chosen field.

As a marine biologist, your career path can take you to various settings: academia, government, private sector, or non-profit organizations. You could become a professor, sharing your passion for marine life with the next generation of scientists. Alternatively, you could work for a government agency, shaping policies and regulations to protect marine habitats and resources. In the private sector, you might join a consultancy firm, advising clients on the environmental impact of their projects. Finally, non-profit organizations offer the chance to work in conservation, advocacy, and public outreach, inspiring others to preserve our oceans for future generations.

The marine biologist's career is not without its challenges. Fieldwork can involve long hours in harsh, remote environments, and securing research funding can be competitive. However, the rewards are immeasurable: witnessing the wonders of the ocean firsthand, contributing to the scientific understanding of marine life, and playing a vital role in conserving our planet's most precious resource.

MARKET RESEARCH ANALYST

A market research analyst plays a critical role in the business world, helping companies better understand their target audiences and discover new opportunities for growth.

At a basic level, a market research analyst is responsible for collecting and analyzing data related to consumer behavior, trends, and preferences. This could involve conducting surveys, focus groups, and other forms of market research to gather data, as well as analyzing sales and financial data to gain insights into market trends and consumer behavior.

Once this data has been collected and analyzed, the market research analyst is then tasked with interpreting the findings and making recommendations to the company based on their insights. For example, they may suggest changes to a company's marketing strategy, product design, or pricing structure based on their understanding of consumer preferences and behaviors.

One interesting aspect of this job is the variety of industries and sectors that market research analysts can work in. These professionals may work for companies in a wide range of fields, including consumer goods, healthcare, technology, finance, and more. This means that a market research analyst's day-to-day tasks and projects could vary widely depending on the specific industry they work in.

Another interesting aspect of this job is the increasing use of data analytics and machine learning in the field of market research. As companies collect more data than ever before, market research analysts are playing an increasingly important role in analyzing and interpreting this data to make informed business decisions. This has led to a growing need for professionals who have both strong analytical skills and a solid understanding of data science and statistical modeling.

In addition to data analysis and interpretation, a market research analyst may also be responsible for developing and executing research plans, managing research projects, and communicating their findings to company executives and other stakeholders. This requires strong project management skills, as well as excellent communication skills and the ability to distill complex data into clear and actionable insights.

Overall, the role of a market research analyst is a fascinating and important one, offering a mix of data analysis, project management, and strategic thinking. It is a great career choice for individuals who enjoy working with data and have a passion for helping companies make informed business decisions based on consumer insights.

MARKETING CREATIVE

A marketing creative's career is a thrilling fusion of imagination, psychology, and strategic communication that ignites consumer interest and drives brand success. Picture yourself crafting captivating stories, designing visuals that demand attention, and devising innovative campaigns that elevate brands above the competition. As a marketing creative, you have the power to shape perceptions, evoke emotions, and inspire consumer action.

The first steps on this exhilarating career journey often involve a solid educational background in marketing, communications, or graphic design. Pursue a Bachelor's degree in one of these fields to gain the foundational knowledge and skills needed to excel as a creative professional. Courses like consumer behavior, brand strategy, and creative design will provide you with insights into the world of marketing and advertising. This is also an excellent time to build your portfolio through internships, freelance work, or collaborations with fellow students.

To sharpen your skills and explore your specific area of interest, consider obtaining a Master's degree or professional certification in marketing, digital marketing, or design. These advanced programs offer a deeper dive into specialized topics such as social media marketing, content creation, or visual storytelling.

The diverse landscape of marketing and advertising offers a wide array of career opportunities for creative professionals. You could work within an advertising agency, joining forces with a team of skilled individuals to develop boundary-pushing campaigns for an eclectic mix of clients. Alternatively, you might choose to work in-house for a company, where you'll help to shape brand identity and forge strong connections with target audiences. For those with entrepreneurial ambitions, freelance work or starting your own marketing consultancy allows for greater flexibility and the chance to engage with a variety of clients and projects.

As a marketing creative, you'll undoubtedly encounter challenges such as demanding deadlines, ever-evolving consumer trends, and the need to stay ahead of new technologies. However, the rewards are both stimulating and fulfilling: witnessing the tangible impact of your work, influencing consumer decisions, and contributing to the growth and success of businesses.

MASTER DISTILLER

A master distiller is a professional who is responsible for the creation of various types of distilled alcoholic beverages. These may include everything from bourbon and whiskey to gin, vodka, and other spirits. The master distiller is responsible for every aspect of the production process, from selecting ingredients and creating recipes to supervising the distillation process and managing the aging of the finished product.

One of the most important aspects of a master distiller's job is recipe development. This involves selecting the raw materials that will be used in the production process, such as grains, fruits, and herbs, and experimenting with different combinations to create unique flavor profiles. This can be a time-consuming and challenging process, as the distiller must balance various factors such as the alcohol content, flavor, and aroma of the finished product.

Once a recipe has been developed, the master distiller oversees the production process itself. This can involve operating complex machinery such as stills, boilers, and tanks, as well as monitoring the temperature and humidity levels to ensure that the distillation process proceeds smoothly. The distiller also carefully monitors the alcohol content of the finished product, adjusting the temperature and other parameters as needed to achieve the desired results.

After the distillation process is complete, the master distiller is responsible for overseeing the aging process of the finished product. This may involve storing the product in barrels for several months or even years, depending on the type of spirit being produced. During this time, the distiller may monitor the temperature and humidity levels of the storage area to ensure that the product is aging properly and developing the desired flavors and aromas.

In addition to these technical skills, a master distiller must also possess a keen sense of taste and smell. This allows them to identify subtle differences in the finished product, such as variations in flavor or aroma, and make adjustments to the production process accordingly. A good distiller must also have a deep knowledge of the history and traditions of the spirits they produce, as well as an understanding of the market for these products and the tastes of their customers.

In recent years, the craft distilling industry has exploded in popularity, and many master distillers have become celebrities in their own right. These professionals are often called upon to represent their brands at events such as festivals, tastings, and trade shows, and may even be featured in documentaries or other media.

MATHEMATICIAN

Mathematics is the study of patterns and structures that can be found in various areas of the universe, from the smallest subatomic particles to the largest galaxies. Mathematicians are professionals who use mathematical principles to solve problems and create new theories.

Mathematicians work in a wide range of fields, including finance, physics, biology, engineering, computer science, and cryptography, among others. They use advanced mathematical concepts, algorithms, and models to develop new solutions to real-world problems. They use mathematical theories to predict the behavior of systems and make recommendations based on their findings.

One of the primary responsibilities of mathematicians is to develop new mathematical models and theories. They use these models to analyze and interpret complex data, create algorithms, and develop new computational methods. They work closely with other scientists and professionals to develop new applications for these models and theories.

In the finance industry, mathematicians use complex models to analyze market data, develop investment strategies, and create risk management plans. These models are used to predict market trends and to identify profitable investment opportunities. They work closely with investment managers, hedge fund managers, and other financial professionals to develop trading strategies that are based on mathematical principles.

In the field of physics, mathematicians use their skills to develop new theories that help us better understand the nature of the universe. They use mathematical models to predict the behavior of subatomic particles, the nature of black holes, and the properties of dark matter.

In computer science, mathematicians use mathematical concepts to develop new algorithms and software applications. They work on a wide range of projects, from developing new encryption methods to creating complex artificial intelligence systems. They also work on projects related to data analysis, machine learning, and computer graphics.

In order to become a mathematician, one must typically have a strong educational background in mathematics or a related field. Many mathematicians also hold advanced degrees in other fields, such as physics, engineering, or computer science.

MECHANICAL ENGINEER

Mechanical engineers are the creative problem solvers of the engineering world. They use their knowledge of mechanics, energy, materials, and design to create new machines and technologies that make our lives easier and more efficient.

As a mechanical engineer, you might work on all kinds of projects, from designing robots that explore other planets to developing renewable energy sources like wind turbines and solar panels. You might also work on more everyday projects, like designing cars or improving the heating and cooling systems in buildings.

One of the coolest things about being a mechanical engineer is that you get to use your creativity and technical skills to solve complex problems. For example, you might be tasked with designing a machine that can perform a certain task, but there are a lot of limitations that you have to work around. You'll need to figure out the best materials to use, the most efficient design, and how to make sure the machine is safe to use.

Mechanical engineers work in a variety of industries, including aerospace, automotive, manufacturing, and energy. They might work in research and development, design, testing, or production. Some even start their own companies and become entrepreneurs.

One thing that sets mechanical engineering apart from other engineering disciplines is the focus on physics and materials science. Mechanical engineers need to understand how forces work, how materials behave under different conditions, and how to design machines that can withstand wear and tear. This means they need to have a deep understanding of physics, math, and materials science.

Another important aspect of mechanical engineering is computer-aided design (CAD) software. This allows engineers to create 3D models of their designs and test them virtually before building physical prototypes. It's a powerful tool that can save a lot of time and money in the design process.

Besides technical skills, mechanical engineers also need to have strong communication and teamwork skills. They often work in multidisciplinary teams with other engineers, scientists, and technicians. They need to be able to explain complex ideas and designs to people who might not have the same technical background as they do.

Overall, mechanical engineering is a challenging and rewarding field that offers endless possibilities for innovation and problem solving. If you're interested in how things work and how to make them work better, a career in mechanical engineering might be right for you.

METEOROLOGIST

A meteorologist's career path is a captivating voyage into the atmospheric wonders of our planet. Imagine yourself decoding the mysteries of weather patterns, forecasting storms that shape the course of history, and investigating the complex dynamics of Earth's climate. As a meteorologist, you will be an interpreter of the skies, wielding the power to predict the elements and protect lives and property from nature's fury.

Embarking on this fascinating career path begins with a robust foundation in the sciences. Aspiring meteorologists should consider pursuing a Bachelor's degree in meteorology, atmospheric science, or a related field. During your undergraduate studies, you'll delve into courses like synoptic meteorology, climatology, and remote sensing, equipping you with the knowledge and skills to understand and forecast weather phenomena. This is also an excellent time to gain practical experience through internships at weather stations, research centers, or government agencies.

To further specialize in your area of interest within meteorology, you might choose to pursue a Master's or Doctorate degree. You could focus on topics such as severe weather, climate change, or air quality, depending on your passion. Graduate programs provide opportunities for hands-on research, allowing you to work closely with faculty members and contribute to the advancement of meteorological science.

Meteorologists can find rewarding careers in various settings, including government agencies, the private sector, academia, and the media. You could work for the National Weather Service or similar organizations, issuing forecasts and warnings to protect the public from hazardous weather conditions. In the private sector, meteorologists play a crucial role in industries like aviation, agriculture, and energy, providing weather insights to optimize operations and mitigate risks. Alternatively, you could become a university professor, conducting research and inspiring the next generation of meteorologists. For those with a flair for communication, broadcasting weather updates on television or radio offers an opportunity to educate and inform the public.

The meteorologist's career is not without its challenges, such as the pressure to produce accurate forecasts or the need to adapt to rapidly evolving technology. However, the rewards are immense: the satisfaction of helping people make informed decisions, contributing to the scientific understanding of our planet's atmosphere, and the thrill of exploring Earth's ever-changing weather systems.

MICROBIOLOGIST

Microbiology is a fascinating field that explores the mysteries of the microscopic world. Microbiologists are scientists who study microorganisms like bacteria, viruses, fungi, and algae. They work to understand how these tiny organisms function and how they interact with their environment.

Microbiologists use a variety of tools and techniques to study microorganisms. They may use microscopes to observe bacteria and viruses or genetic sequencing to analyze the genetic makeup of an organism. They also use lab equipment like centrifuges, petri dishes, and pipettes to manipulate and grow microorganisms.

One of the key areas of focus for microbiologists is understanding the role microorganisms play in the natural world. They study how microbes help break down dead organic matter, release nutrients into the soil, and interact with other organisms in their environment. This knowledge is important for understanding ecosystems, and for developing strategies for managing environmental health.

Another area of focus for microbiologists is the role of microorganisms in human health. Microbes can cause a wide range of diseases, from the common cold to life-threatening infections. Microbiologists work to understand how these pathogens function, and to develop new treatments and vaccines to combat them.

In addition to disease-causing microbes, microbiologists also study the beneficial bacteria that live in and on our bodies. These microbes are essential to our health, helping us to digest food, produce vitamins, and support our immune system. By studying the microbiome, microbiologists hope to better understand how these bacteria function and how we can support them for optimal health.

Microbiologists work in a variety of settings, from universities and research institutions to government agencies and private industry. Some microbiologists work in the field, collecting samples from the natural world, while others work exclusively in the lab. They may also work with other scientists, such as chemists and engineers, to develop new technologies and tools for studying microorganisms.

There are many different areas of specialization within microbiology. Some microbiologists specialize in studying specific types of organisms, like bacteria or viruses. Others focus on particular environments, such as marine or soil microbiology. There are also microbiologists who specialize in public health, agriculture, or industrial processes like food production or bioremediation.

MINING ENGINEER

Embarking on a career as a mining engineer is like venturing into an underground labyrinth filled with untapped treasures. As a mining engineer, you'll be the ingenious mastermind behind the safe and efficient extraction of Earth's valuable resources. With each project, you'll contribute to the foundation of modern society and help shape the future of the global economy.

The first steps toward becoming a mining engineer involve acquiring a strong STEM background. Obtain a Bachelor's degree in mining engineering, geological engineering, or a related field to immerse yourself in subjects like mineralogy, geotechnics, and mine design.

Advanced degrees, such as a Master's or Doctorate, can open doors to specialized fields within mining engineering. By pursuing further education, you'll have the opportunity to focus on areas like mineral processing, rock mechanics, or sustainable mining practices. Graduate studies also offer valuable research experience, enabling you to work closely with seasoned engineers and make meaningful contributions to the field.

The mining engineering profession boasts a diverse range of career opportunities. You might find yourself working for private mining companies, consulting firms, or government organizations. As a field engineer, you'll supervise mine operations and ensure worker safety, while office-based roles may involve planning and designing mining projects.

Despite the challenges that come with balancing profitability and sustainability, a mining engineer's career is incredibly rewarding. You'll take pride in unearthing Earth's hidden gems, contributing to the economy, and promoting responsible resource management.

Mining engineers are akin to subterranean treasure hunters, digging into the depths of the Earth and unearthing the resources that power our world. They are the creative thinkers who devise innovative extraction methods, the guardians of responsible resource management, and the pioneers shaping the future of the mining industry. If your curiosity is piqued by the geological wonders beneath our feet, and you're driven by the desire to create a tangible impact on society, a career as a mining engineer offers an extraordinary journey marked by discovery, innovation, and the opportunity to leave a lasting imprint on the world.

MOBILE APP DEVELOPER

Diving into a career as a mobile app developer is like stepping onto a fast-paced roller coaster through the ever-changing world of technology. As a mobile app developer, you'll be the ingenious architect crafting applications that entertain, educate, and simplify life for people across the globe. With each app you create, you'll not only redefine the way users engage with their devices but also contribute to the fast-paced evolution of the tech landscape.

To kick-start your journey, develop a strong background in computer science and programming. Obtain a Bachelor's degree in computer science, software engineering, or a related discipline to build your knowledge of programming languages, algorithms, and data structures. Your academic adventure will introduce you to courses such as mobile app development, user experience (UX) design, and software architecture. Complement your formal education with internships and personal projects to amass a diverse portfolio that highlights your skills and creativity.

In the expansive world of mobile app development, finding a niche or specializing in a particular platform can be a game-changer for your career. You may opt to focus on iOS or Android app development or delve into specialized app categories like gaming, productivity, or fitness. To sharpen your skills, pursue platform-specific certifications, enroll in targeted courses, or attend industry events and workshops.

A multitude of exhilarating career avenues await mobile app developers across various sectors, including tech giants, startups, government entities, and non-profits. As an in-house developer, you'll join forces with a team to design and maintain apps for a diverse clientele. Freelance developers, on the other hand, can offer their expertise on a project-by-project basis. If the entrepreneurial path calls your name, consider launching your own app or establishing a development company to realize your unique vision.

While the competitive mobile app market and the necessity to stay abreast of emerging technologies present challenges, the rewards are abundant. As a mobile app developer, you'll relish the fulfillment of transforming ideas into tangible products, influencing how people interact with technology, and leaving your mark on the digital world.

MUSIC PRODUCER

A music producer is responsible for overseeing the creation of music. They work with artists and other music professionals to create, record, and produce songs and albums. The role of a music producer is multi-faceted, and can include everything from conceptualizing the overall sound of a project to overseeing the mixing and mastering process.

A music producer's job starts long before the first note is played or the first word is sung. They work with the artist to help them develop their sound and define their artistic vision. This can include selecting songs, arranging instrumentation, and choosing the right recording studio. A good music producer will help an artist create their best possible work, while staying true to their unique style and creative vision.

Once the music is ready to be recorded, the music producer is responsible for overseeing the recording process. This involves working with the musicians to ensure that they are playing their parts correctly and that the sound is being captured correctly. They may work with the sound engineer to adjust levels, add effects, and create a cohesive sound.

After the recording process is complete, the music producer is responsible for overseeing the mixing and mastering process. Mixing involves taking all of the individual tracks and combining them into a single, cohesive sound. This can involve adjusting levels, adding effects, and tweaking the overall sound to achieve the desired result. Mastering involves taking the final mix and making it sound its best by adjusting the levels, adding final effects, and preparing the music for release.

Music producers often work with a team of other professionals, including recording engineers, mixing engineers, session musicians, and mastering engineers. They need to be able to communicate effectively with all of these people and ensure that everyone is working together toward the same goal.

One of the most important skills for a music producer is the ability to listen. They need to be able to listen to an artist's ideas, to the music that is being created, and to feedback from other professionals. They need to be able to use this feedback to make adjustments and to ensure that the music is as good as it can be.

MUSICIAN

A musician's career is like stepping into a colorful world of sound, where you'll create music that touches hearts and unites people. As a musician, you'll use rhythm, melody, and emotion to make memorable experiences, making your mark on the ever-changing world of music.

Your path as a musician starts with learning your chosen instrument or voice and having a deep love for music. A Bachelor's degree in music performance, composition, or music education can give you a strong base in music theory, history, and technique. Alongside your studies, explore different musical styles and genres, improving your skills through practice, performing, and working with other artists.

While formal education is helpful, a musician's journey is often shaped by personal growth, various experiences, and a strong dedication to the craft. Attend workshops, masterclasses, and music camps to learn from professionals and sharpen your skills. Networking is crucial, so participate in local music scenes, open mics, and festivals to make connections and gain exposure.

A musician's career offers many opportunities to showcase your talent and creativity. You might perform as a solo artist, in a band, or as part of an orchestra, connecting with live audiences and recording albums. You could also compose music for films, TV, video games, or other artists. Music educators play an essential role in helping the next generation of musicians through private lessons, school programs, or community projects.

A musician's career can be challenging, with industry uncertainties or the need for recognition. However, the rewards are incredibly fulfilling. As a musician, you'll enjoy connecting with audiences, the excitement of artistic exploration, and the satisfaction of contributing to human expression.

Musicians are the skilled artists who guide us through various emotions and the creative composers who make beautiful soundscapes. They preserve cultural heritage, explore new musical ideas, and inspire us to dream, dance, and feel. If you love the magic of music, want to express yourself, and share your gift with the world, a career as a musician offers a fantastic journey filled with harmony, adventure, and the chance to touch many lives through the power of sound.

NEUROLOGIST

A neurologist is a medical doctor who specializes in treating disorders of the nervous system, which includes the brain, spinal cord, and nerves throughout the body. The nervous system is a complex network that controls our thoughts, movements, sensations, and functions of the body's organs. Neurologists work to diagnose, treat, and manage a wide range of conditions that affect the nervous system.

One of the primary responsibilities of a neurologist is diagnosing and treating neurological disorders. Six of the most common conditions that neurologists diagnose and treat include: epilepsy, Alzheimer's disease, Parkinson's disease, multiple sclerosis, migraines, and strokes. They use a variety of techniques and tests, such as magnetic resonance imaging (MRI), computed tomography (CT) scans, electroencephalograms (EEGs), and nerve conduction studies, to help identify and diagnose these conditions.

Neurologists also work to manage and treat neurological conditions to improve the quality of life for their patients. This may involve prescribing medication, providing physical therapy, or recommending lifestyle changes. They work closely with other healthcare providers, including physical therapists, occupational therapists, speech therapists, and social workers, to develop a comprehensive treatment plan that addresses their patients' needs.

In addition to treating individual patients, neurologists also conduct research to better understand the mechanisms behind neurological diseases and develop new treatments. They may conduct clinical trials to test the effectiveness of new medications or therapies, or study the genetic and environmental factors that contribute to neurological disorders.

Another important aspect of the work of neurologists is patient education. They work to educate patients and their families about their conditions, how to manage their symptoms, and what to expect during treatment.

Neurologists work in a variety of settings, including hospitals, clinics, private practices, and research institutions. They work closely with other healthcare providers, including primary care physicians, neurosurgeons, psychiatrists, and nurses, to provide comprehensive care to their patients.

One of the most fascinating aspects of neurology is the ability of the brain to adapt and change over time. Neurologists work to understand the mechanisms behind this plasticity, and how it can be harnessed to improve the lives of patients. For example, they may use techniques such as neuroplasticity-based therapies to help patients recover from traumatic brain injuries or strokes.

NUCLEAR SCIENTIST

Nuclear science is a fascinating and complex field that encompasses a range of applications, from energy generation to medical treatments to nuclear weapons. Nuclear scientists are the experts who specialize in this area, and their work is diverse and essential.

A nuclear scientist is a professional who studies the properties and behavior of atomic nuclei and the particles that make them up. They are responsible for developing and testing theories and models of atomic structure, developing new technologies that utilize nuclear processes, and designing and maintaining nuclear facilities.

One of the main areas of study for nuclear scientists is nuclear physics. This branch of physics is concerned with the structure and behavior of atomic nuclei and the particles that make them up. Nuclear physicists use complex mathematical models and advanced experimental techniques to study the properties of atomic nuclei and to understand the fundamental nature of matter and energy.

Another important area of study for nuclear scientists is nuclear engineering. This field involves the design, construction, and maintenance of nuclear reactors and other nuclear facilities. Nuclear engineers work to develop new technologies that can improve the efficiency and safety of nuclear power generation, as well as to address the many challenges associated with nuclear waste management and decommissioning.

Medical physics is also an important area of study for nuclear scientists. This field involves the use of nuclear technologies in medical treatments and diagnosis, such as radiation therapy for cancer and the use of nuclear imaging techniques like PET and MRI. Medical physicists work closely with doctors and other healthcare professionals to develop new treatments and technologies that can help to improve patient outcomes and quality of life.

In addition to their research and development work, nuclear scientists also play a vital role in ensuring the safety and security of nuclear materials and facilities. They work with government agencies and private organizations to develop and enforce regulations and protocols that protect the public and the environment from the dangers of nuclear materials and technologies.

Overall, the work of a nuclear scientist is incredibly important and fascinating. These professionals play a crucial role in advancing our understanding of the fundamental nature of matter and energy, developing new technologies that can improve our lives, and ensuring the safety and security of nuclear materials and facilities.

NURSE

Nurses are very important and definitely key people in the medical industry. They are responsible for providing care to patients in hospitals, clinics, and other medical facilities. Nurses are vital members of a healthcare team, and they play a critical role in patient care, monitoring and assessing patients, providing medications, and educating patients and their families about their care.

A nurse's responsibilities depend on their area of specialization. Registered Nurses (RNs) are the largest group of nurses and have various areas of expertise. They may work in a general medical setting, such as a hospital or clinic, or specialize in fields such as pediatrics, geriatrics, oncology, or emergency medicine. RNs work closely with physicians and other healthcare professionals to provide coordinated and comprehensive care to patients.

In addition to providing direct patient care, nurses also manage and coordinate care for patients. They work with the healthcare team to develop and implement treatment plans, and they provide education and support to patients and their families. Nurses may also supervise other healthcare staff, such as nursing assistants and LPNs.

One of the most important roles of a nurse is to assess and monitor patients. Nurses use their knowledge of patient care and medical technology to monitor patients' vital signs, including blood pressure, heart rate, respiratory rate, and temperature. They also evaluate patient symptoms, track their medical history, and communicate with doctors and other healthcare professionals to adjust treatment plans as necessary.

In addition to medical knowledge, nurses must have excellent communication skills. They must communicate effectively with patients, their families, and other healthcare professionals. They must be able to provide clear and concise instructions to patients and answer questions about their care.

Nurses also play an important role in preventing the spread of disease. They are responsible for taking appropriate precautions to protect themselves and others from infectious diseases. They follow strict protocols for hand hygiene, wear appropriate personal protective equipment, and take other measures to prevent the spread of germs.

Nurses are also advocates for their patients. They act as the patient's voice, ensuring that their needs are met and that their rights are protected. They help patients and their families understand their healthcare options and support them in making informed decisions about their care.

NUTRITIONIST

Nutritionists are professionals who specialize in the study of nutrition and its effects on human health. They work with clients to create individualized nutrition plans based on their health goals, dietary needs, and medical history. Nutritionists often work in a variety of settings, including hospitals, clinics, gyms, schools, and private practices.

The primary responsibility of a nutritionist is to help clients achieve optimal health through proper nutrition. This includes educating clients about the nutritional value of various foods, developing meal plans based on their individual needs, and monitoring their progress over time. Nutritionists work with clients to develop healthy eating habits, which may include increasing intake of certain nutrients, decreasing intake of others, or making other dietary changes to achieve their goals.

In addition to working with individual clients, nutritionists may also work with healthcare providers to develop nutrition plans for patients with medical conditions. For example, a nutritionist may work with a team of healthcare providers to develop a meal plan for a patient with diabetes or heart disease.

One of the most important roles of a nutritionist is to stay up-to-date with the latest research in the field of nutrition. This involves reading scientific studies, attending conferences and workshops, and staying informed about the latest dietary trends and fads.

In order to become a nutritionist, a person typically needs to earn a bachelor's degree in nutrition or a related field, although some states require additional education and training to become licensed or certified.

One of the most interesting aspects of being a nutritionist is the ability to help people make positive changes in their lives through diet and lifestyle changes. Another interesting aspect of being a nutritionist is the variety of career paths available. In addition to working in traditional settings such as hospitals and clinics, nutritionists may also work in research, education, sports nutrition, public health, and more.

Finally, nutritionists have the opportunity to make a real difference in the lives of their clients. By helping people make positive changes in their diets and lifestyles, nutritionists can help prevent and manage a variety of chronic diseases, including diabetes, heart disease, and obesity.

OCCUPATIONAL THERAPIST

An occupational therapist (OT) is a healthcare professional who helps people of all ages to participate in daily activities that are important to them. Occupational therapy is a type of rehabilitation that uses meaningful activities to promote health and wellbeing, prevent disability, and enhance quality of life.

OTs work with people who have physical, developmental, emotional, or cognitive challenges that impact their ability to perform everyday tasks. This could include anything from a child with autism who has difficulty with social interactions, to an older adult who has suffered a stroke and needs to re-learn how to dress themselves.

To help their clients, OTs begin by conducting an evaluation to assess their abilities and needs. Based on this assessment, they develop a customized treatment plan that may include exercises, activities, and modifications to the person's environment or equipment to support their functional goals.

For example, an occupational therapist might help a child with sensory processing issues to better tolerate different textures, smells, or sounds by using a variety of sensory experiences, like touching different textures or listening to calming music. Alternatively, an OT working with a person who has had a stroke may help them practice everyday activities like dressing, cooking, or using the bathroom, using adaptive equipment and techniques to support their independence.

OTs work in a wide range of settings, including hospitals, schools, rehabilitation centers, community centers, and private practice. They collaborate with other healthcare professionals, like physicians, physical therapists, and speech therapists, to provide comprehensive care.

In addition to providing direct patient care, OTs also educate their clients, families, and caregivers on how to safely perform activities of daily living, promote health and wellness, and prevent further injury or illness. They also advocate for their clients, ensuring that they have access to necessary resources and accommodations to support their participation in society.

Occupational therapy is a rewarding career that requires a strong foundation in science, creativity, and problem-solving. It offers the opportunity to make a meaningful difference in the lives of people facing physical, emotional, and cognitive challenges.

OCEANOGRAPHER

The career path of an oceanographer involves navigating into the complex and vast world of Earth's oceans, where one strives to uncover the intricacies of marine ecosystems and their relationship with the environment. As an oceanographer, you will investigate the various aspects of the oceans, analyze the interactions between marine life and their surroundings, and contribute to the preservation of our planet's most vital resource.

To initiate your career as an oceanographer, it is essential to establish a robust foundation in the sciences. Obtain a Bachelor's degree in oceanography, marine biology, or a related discipline to gain comprehensive knowledge in fields such as marine geology, chemistry, and physics. Throughout your education, you will examine ocean currents, ecosystems, and the influence of human activities on marine habitats. Participate in internships, research projects, and fieldwork to acquire practical experience and hone your expertise.

Given the diverse nature of oceanography, specialization in a particular subfield can prove advantageous for your career. Potential areas of focus include biological, chemical, geological, or physical oceanography, each providing unique perspectives on marine environments. Pursuing advanced degrees, such as a Master's or Doctorate, can further deepen your understanding of the subject and enable you to contribute significantly to the field through research and innovation.

Various sectors offer intriguing career opportunities for oceanographers, including government agencies, research institutions, universities, and private corporations. In a research scientist role, you will examine the intricate dynamics of marine environments, assess the effects of climate change on oceans, and contribute to the formulation of sustainable practices. Academic positions provide the opportunity to nurture the upcoming generation of oceanographers and impart your enthusiasm for marine studies.

Although a career in oceanography can be demanding, with extensive fieldwork and the necessity to remain updated on scientific advancements, the rewards are profoundly gratifying. As an oceanographer, your efforts will contribute to the comprehension and conservation of our oceans, address crucial environmental challenges, and have a lasting impact on the well-being of our planet.

In conclusion, oceanographers are the dedicated explorers of Earth's immense oceans and the innovative problem-solvers dedicated to their protection.

OFFICE MANAGER

An office manager is a professional who takes care of the efficient operation and management of an office or workplace. They are the backbone of any organization, providing essential administrative support that ensures the smooth running of daily operations. Office managers are typically responsible for supervising administrative staff, maintaining office equipment and supplies, and ensuring that office policies and procedures are followed.

Office managers must have excellent organizational skills, as they are responsible for maintaining schedules and calendars, coordinating meetings, and handling a wide range of administrative tasks. They must also be able to communicate effectively, both orally and in writing, as they interact with employees, clients, and other stakeholders on a daily basis. Other essential skills include problem-solving, time management, and attention to detail.

One of the most important roles of an office manager is to supervise administrative staff and ensure that they are performing their duties effectively. This includes hiring, training, and evaluating staff members, as well as assigning tasks and monitoring their performance. Office managers are also responsible for ensuring that office equipment and supplies are in good working order and that they are available when needed. They may also be responsible for managing office finances, including budgeting and accounting tasks.

In addition to managing administrative tasks, office managers are also responsible for creating and maintaining office policies and procedures. This may include developing new policies, revising existing policies, and ensuring that all employees are aware of and follow these policies. They must also ensure that the office is in compliance with all relevant laws and regulations.

Office managers may also be responsible for managing the physical space of the office. This includes ensuring that the office is clean, well-maintained, and safe. They may also be responsible for organizing and maintaining files, records, and other important documents.

Overall, office managers are essential to the smooth running of any organization. They play a vital role in managing administrative tasks, supervising staff, and maintaining the overall organization of the workplace. If you enjoy working in a fast-paced environment and have excellent organizational and communication skills, a career as an office manager may be a good fit for you.

ONCOLOGIST

An oncologist is a medical professional who specializes in the diagnosis and treatment of cancer. They work with patients who have been diagnosed with cancer, helping them navigate the complex and often daunting process of cancer treatment.

To become an oncologist, one must first obtain a medical degree and then complete a residency in internal medicine or a related field. After completing their residency, they must complete additional training in oncology, which can take several years.

Oncologists work in a variety of settings, including hospitals, clinics, and research facilities. They work closely with other medical professionals, such as surgeons and radiologists, to provide comprehensive care to cancer patients.

The role of an oncologist is complex and multifaceted. They must be able to perform a variety of tasks, including:

1. Diagnosing cancer: Oncologists use a variety of tools and tests to diagnose cancer. They may perform physical exams, order lab tests or imaging tests such as CT scans, PET scans or MRIs, and conduct biopsies to collect tissue samples.

2. Determining the stage and type of cancer: Once a cancer diagnosis is made, oncologists work to determine the stage and type of cancer. This information is important in deciding the best treatment approach.

3. Developing a treatment plan: Oncologists work with other medical professionals to develop a comprehensive treatment plan for their patients. This may include surgery, radiation therapy, chemotherapy, or other types of treatment.

4. Managing treatment side effects: Cancer treatment can be very challenging, and oncologists must work closely with their patients to manage the side effects of treatment.

5. Providing emotional support: A cancer diagnosis can be very difficult for patients and their families. Oncologists must be able to provide emotional support and guidance to their patients, helping them cope with the challenges of treatment and navigate the complex emotions that come with a cancer diagnosis.

6. Conducting research: Many oncologists are also involved in research, working to advance our understanding of cancer and develop new treatments for the disease.

The work of an oncologist is rewarding, and essential. By working to diagnose and treat cancer, oncologists play a vital role in helping patients live longer, healthier lives.

OPTOMETRIST

Optometrists are medical professionals who specialize in diagnosing and treating various eye-related issues. They take care of patients of all ages to ensure that their eyes are healthy and functioning properly. Optometrists can help patients with a variety of vision problems, from nearsightedness and farsightedness to more serious conditions like cataracts and glaucoma.

One of the main duties of an optometrist is to perform eye exams. During these exams, the optometrist will evaluate a patient's eyes for signs of disease, injury, or other problems. They will also assess the patient's visual acuity, or how well they can see, and determine if the patient needs glasses or contact lenses. Optometrists use a variety of tools and techniques to examine the eyes, including a slit lamp microscope, an ophthalmoscope, and a retinoscope.

Another important task that optometrists perform is prescribing glasses and contact lenses. They will work with patients to find the best possible lenses for their specific vision needs, taking into account factors like the patient's age, occupation, and lifestyle. Optometrists will also provide guidance on how to properly care for glasses and contact lenses, and offer tips on how to avoid eye strain from prolonged computer use.

In addition to prescribing glasses and contact lenses, optometrists can also provide treatment for a variety of eye conditions. This may include prescribing medication, recommending eye exercises, or referring patients to other medical specialists if necessary. Optometrists may also perform minor surgical procedures, such as removing foreign objects from the eye.

One of the unique aspects of optometry is the ability to work in a variety of settings. Many optometrists work in private practices or optometry clinics, but others may work in hospitals or other healthcare facilities. Some optometrists even work in research or academic settings, studying the latest advancements in vision care and developing new treatments for eye-related conditions.

In order to become an optometrist, an individual must complete a four-year Doctor of Optometry (OD) degree program, which includes both classroom instruction and clinical training. After earning their degree, optometrists must pass a licensure exam in order to practice in their state.

ORTHODONTIST

An orthodontist is a type of dentist who specializes in the alignment and positioning of teeth and jaws. They are responsible for helping people achieve a beautiful, healthy smile by correcting dental and orthodontic problems.

Orthodontists work with patients of all ages, from young children to adults, to address a variety of issues such as crowded or crooked teeth, overbites and underbites, and jaw problems. They use a variety of tools and techniques to move teeth into their correct position and ensure a proper bite.

One of the most common tools an orthodontist uses is braces. Braces are small metal or ceramic brackets that are attached to the teeth and connected by a thin wire. Over time, the wire is tightened, which gradually moves the teeth into their correct position. While braces are the most well-known orthodontic treatment, there are other options available as well, including clear aligners, lingual braces (which are placed on the back of the teeth), and self-ligating braces.

In addition to straightening teeth, orthodontists also work to correct problems with the bite. An improper bite can cause problems with speech, chewing, and even breathing. By adjusting the position of the teeth and jaws, orthodontists can help improve these issues and promote proper jaw growth and development.

Orthodontists also work closely with other dental professionals, such as general dentists, periodontists, and oral surgeons, to ensure their patients receive comprehensive care. They may also provide education and guidance to help patients maintain their oral health and keep their teeth and gums healthy throughout their lives.

To become an orthodontist, one must first complete a dental degree and become a licensed dentist. From there, they must complete additional specialized training in orthodontics, which can take two to three years or more. Orthodontists must also stay up to date on the latest techniques and technologies in the field, and maintain a commitment to ongoing education and professional development.

For young people who are interested in becoming an orthodontist, it's important to have a love of science and an interest in working with people. Good communication skills and attention to detail are also important traits for success in this field. By pursuing a career as an orthodontist, you can help people achieve a healthy, confident smile that they will be proud to show off!

PAINTER

A painter is an artist who specializes in creating visual images through the use of color pigments, brushstrokes, and various techniques on different surfaces such as canvas, paper, wood, or walls. Painters use a wide range of tools to create their art, including brushes, palettes, and paint. They may work with oil, acrylic, watercolor, or other mediums to create their masterpieces.

Painters often begin their work by studying the subject they plan to paint. They may use photographs, live models, or their imagination to create the initial sketches for their artwork. Once they have a general idea of what they want to create, painters begin the actual painting process. This typically involves applying multiple layers of paint to the surface, allowing each layer to dry before adding the next. They may use a variety of techniques, such as blending, shading, and layering, to create the desired effect.

In addition to creating art, many painters also work on commercial projects such as murals or advertising displays. These projects often involve working with a team of designers, marketers, and other professionals to create a cohesive message or image. Painters may be responsible for creating the initial sketches, selecting the appropriate colors and materials, and overseeing the installation or display of the final product.

Beyond commercial work, painters may also pursue a career as a fine artist. This typically involves creating unique pieces of art that are sold through galleries, exhibitions, or other venues. Fine artists often work independently, creating their own vision without the constraints of a client or commercial project.

To be successful as a painter, one must have a keen eye for color, form, and composition. They must also possess a strong sense of creativity and the ability to work independently. Patience, attention to detail, and the ability to work for long periods of time are also important traits for painters.

In addition to creating art, painters may also be responsible for maintaining their tools and equipment. They must ensure that their brushes, paints, and other materials are clean and properly stored to prevent damage or contamination. Painters must also be familiar with safety practices, such as using ventilation when working with certain chemicals or materials.

PARALEGAL

Paralegals are an essential part of the legal system, and they help lawyers in many different ways. They work in law firms, corporations, government agencies, and other organizations that require legal services. Paralegals play an important role in assisting attorneys with legal research, drafting legal documents, interviewing clients, and managing case files. They also provide general support to attorneys during trials, hearings, and other legal proceedings.

One of the main tasks of a paralegal is to assist attorneys with legal research. This involves finding and analyzing legal information such as case law, statutes, and regulations. Paralegals use online databases, law libraries, and other resources to conduct legal research and provide attorneys with the information they need to make informed decisions.

Paralegals also assist with drafting legal documents, including pleadings, motions, and briefs. They work closely with attorneys to ensure that these documents are accurate and complete, and they may even be responsible for filing them with the court.

Another important task that paralegals perform is interviewing clients and witnesses. They help attorneys prepare for depositions and trials by gathering information from clients and witnesses and organizing it in a clear and concise manner. Paralegals may also attend depositions and trials to provide support to attorneys.

Paralegals also manage case files, which can be quite complex and voluminous. They organize documents, track deadlines, and ensure that all relevant information is easily accessible to the legal team. Paralegals may also be responsible for communicating with opposing counsel, court personnel, and clients.

In addition to these core duties, paralegals may also specialize in a particular area of law, such as corporate law, family law, or intellectual property law. Depending on their specialization, paralegals may perform additional tasks, such as drafting contracts, conducting trademark searches, or preparing estate planning documents.

To become a paralegal, a person typically needs to have a bachelor's degree and complete a paralegal certificate program or an associate's degree in paralegal studies. Some paralegals also have a background in a related field, such as criminal justice or political science. Paralegals must be highly organized and detail-oriented, and they must possess excellent communication skills, both written and verbal.

PARK RANGER

Park rangers are people who work to protect and preserve natural areas, such as national parks, state parks, and wildlife reserves. They are responsible for maintaining the natural beauty and ecological balance of these areas, while also ensuring the safety and enjoyment of visitors.

A park ranger's job can vary depending on their specific role and location, but some of their duties might include:

- Protecting wildlife and habitats: Park rangers work to ensure the safety and health of wildlife and the ecosystems they live in. They may monitor the behavior of animals, help to rehabilitate injured wildlife, and work to prevent poaching and other illegal activities.

- Maintaining trails and facilities: Park rangers are responsible for keeping trails and other recreational areas in good condition. They may clear debris from hiking paths, repair signs and buildings, and maintain other facilities such as campgrounds.

- Providing information and assistance to visitors: Park rangers are often the primary source of information for visitors to natural areas. They may help visitors plan hikes, suggest safe areas for swimming or picnicking, or give advice on what wildlife to watch out for.

- Conducting search and rescue operations: In the event of an emergency, such as a hiker getting lost or injured, park rangers may work to coordinate search and rescue efforts.

- Collaborating with other organizations and agencies: Park rangers often work closely with other organizations and government agencies to manage and protect natural areas. For example, they may work with wildlife biologists to track the movements of animals or collaborate with local law enforcement to prevent illegal activities.

To become a park ranger, you typically need a bachelor's degree in a related field, such as forestry, environmental science, or wildlife management. Many park rangers also have experience working in related fields, such as law enforcement or search and rescue operations. Additionally, park rangers must pass rigorous physical and mental fitness tests, and undergo extensive training in safety, first aid, and environmental protection.

PATENT AGENT

A patent agent is a professional who helps inventors and businesses protect their intellectual property. Intellectual property is a term used to describe any original creation of the mind, such as inventions, literary and artistic works, and symbols and designs.

Patent agents work specifically with inventors and businesses to help them obtain patents for their inventions. A patent is a legal document that gives the holder the exclusive right to make, use, and sell their invention for a certain period of time.

So, what does a patent agent actually do? There are a few key tasks that are typically associated with this profession:

1. Conducting patent searches: One of the first things a patent agent will do is conduct a search to determine whether the invention in question is eligible for a patent. They will also look to see if there are any similar patents that already exist.

2. Preparing and filing patent applications: If the patent agent determines that an invention is eligible for a patent, they will then work to prepare and file a patent application. This involves writing a detailed description of the invention and its use, and submitting the application to the appropriate government agency.

3. Advising on patent strategy: Patent agents may also work with inventors and businesses to help them develop a patent strategy. This might involve advising them on the types of patents that would be most beneficial for their particular situation, or helping them to navigate the patent process in a way that maximizes their chances of success.

Patent agents typically have a strong background in science or engineering, as well as an understanding of intellectual property law. They may work for law firms, corporations, or government agencies, or may operate as independent consultants.

One of the most rewarding aspects of being a patent agent is helping inventors and businesses to protect their ideas and innovations. It can be incredibly satisfying to help a client navigate the patent process and ultimately obtain a patent that protects their hard work and creativity.

If you're interested in becoming a patent agent, it's important to have a strong foundation in science or engineering, as well as excellent research and writing skills. You'll also need to be comfortable working with complex legal concepts and regulations, and have a strong attention to detail.

PEDIATRICIAN

Pediatricians are medical doctors who specialize in the care of infants, children, and adolescents. They play a critical role in keeping children healthy, both physically and mentally, and work to prevent and treat illnesses and injuries that can impact children at every stage of their growth and development.

To become a pediatrician, one must first complete a four-year undergraduate degree followed by four years of medical school. After obtaining a medical degree, aspiring pediatricians must complete a three-year pediatric residency program, during which time they gain hands-on experience in a variety of clinical settings.

Once licensed, pediatricians may work in a variety of settings, including private practice, hospitals, clinics, and community health centers. They are trained to provide a wide range of medical services, including routine check-ups, vaccinations, and sick visits for children of all ages.

One of the most important aspects of a pediatrician's job is preventive care. Pediatricians work closely with parents to ensure that children are developing properly and meeting important developmental milestones. They also help parents establish healthy habits that can prevent the onset of diseases later in life.

Pediatricians are also trained to diagnose and treat a wide range of illnesses and medical conditions that can affect children. This includes everything from common childhood illnesses like the flu and ear infections to more serious conditions such as asthma, diabetes, and cancer. They may also refer children to specialists when needed for more specialized care.

Another important aspect of a pediatrician's work is helping children cope with the emotional and psychological challenges that can arise during childhood and adolescence. They may provide guidance and support for children who are struggling with mental health issues, behavioral problems, or other challenges.

In addition to providing medical care to children, pediatricians also work to promote child health and safety in their communities. They may work with schools, community organizations, and other groups to promote healthy habits for children.

Pediatricians must also stay up-to-date on the latest research and medical practices in their field, as new treatments and technologies are constantly being developed. This requires ongoing education and professional development to ensure that they are providing the highest quality care to their patients.

PERFUMER

Perfumers are artists who create unique and evocative fragrances using a blend of natural and synthetic ingredients. They are often referred to as "noses," due to their exceptional sense of smell and the ability to recognize and identify hundreds of different scent molecules.

Creating a new perfume is a complex and often lengthy process that involves extensive research, experimentation, and a deep understanding of the chemistry and physics of fragrance. A perfumer's job is to develop a new fragrance or to tweak existing ones, to create a scent that meets the needs of a particular client or brand.

One of the primary responsibilities of a perfumer is to carefully select and combine different scent molecules to create a new fragrance. This process involves using a vast array of different ingredients, including natural essences such as flower petals, leaves, and bark, as well as synthetic ingredients such as aldehydes and esters. A perfumer's sense of smell is so refined that they are able to distinguish between different ingredients and to identify their unique scents, even in very small quantities.

In addition to creating new fragrances, perfumers are also responsible for evaluating and testing the quality of existing fragrances. This may involve working with a team of chemists and other specialists to analyze the composition of a fragrance, or conducting sensory evaluations to assess the strength, longevity, and overall appeal of a scent.

Perfumers also work with marketing and branding teams to develop new products, to establish a brand's identity, and to create effective advertising campaigns. This involves understanding the target audience and developing fragrances that will resonate with them. For example, a perfume designed for a young, trendy audience may have a lighter, fresher scent, while a fragrance aimed at an older, more sophisticated audience may have a deeper, more complex scent profile.

Another important aspect of a perfumer's job is keeping up-to-date with the latest fragrance trends and developments in the industry. This involves attending trade shows, keeping tabs on emerging brands, and staying informed about new ingredients and manufacturing techniques.

Becoming a perfumer requires extensive education and training in the art of fragrance composition. Most perfumers start by studying chemistry or a related field, and then go on to pursue specialized training in fragrance development. This may involve attending a specialized fragrance school, working as an apprentice to an experienced perfumer, or participating in industry-sponsored training programs.

PERSONAL CHEF

Do you ever watch cooking shows on TV or help your parents make dinner at home? If so, you might be interested in learning more about what a personal chef does!

A personal chef is a culinary professional who is hired by individuals or families to create customized meals in the client's home or another location. They work closely with clients to create menus based on their specific dietary needs, preferences, and tastes. Personal chefs typically use high-quality ingredients to create meals that are not only healthy, but also delicious and visually appealing.

One of the great things about being a personal chef is the opportunity to be creative. They get to experiment with different flavors, ingredients, and cooking techniques to create unique dishes that their clients will love. In addition, personal chefs must be knowledgeable about a variety of cuisines, including international and regional specialties, to meet the diverse needs of their clients.

Here are some of the key responsibilities and duties of a personal chef:

1. Menu planning: Personal chefs work with clients to develop menus based on their dietary preferences and restrictions, as well as the occasion (e.g., a dinner party, a family gathering, or everyday meals). They also take into consideration the client's budget and available ingredients.

2. Shopping: Personal chefs often shop for ingredients for their clients, selecting high-quality and fresh items to use in their cooking. This means they need to have a good understanding of where to find the best ingredients and how to select them.

3. Meal preparation: Once the menu is established and the ingredients are purchased, personal chefs begin preparing the meals. This can include everything from chopping vegetables to preparing sauces to grilling meats. They often work alone in the client's kitchen, but may also work with a team of assistants.

4. Presentation: In addition to cooking, personal chefs are responsible for making the meals visually appealing. They must use their creativity and knowledge of plating techniques to present the food in an aesthetically pleasing way.

To become a personal chef, you typically need to have a strong background in culinary arts, including formal training and/or experience working in a professional kitchen.

PERSONAL TRAINER

A personal trainer is a fitness professional who helps people achieve their fitness goals. They work with individuals or small groups to develop and implement exercise plans that are tailored to their clients' needs and abilities.

One of the key roles of a personal trainer is to motivate and inspire their clients. They help people set realistic and achievable fitness goals, and then provide the guidance, support, and accountability that is needed to reach those goals.

Personal trainers may work with clients of all ages and fitness levels, and they may specialize in a particular area of fitness such as weight loss, strength training, or athletic performance. They may work in a gym or fitness center, or they may provide in-home training services.

Some of the specific duties of a personal trainer might include:

- Conducting fitness assessments: This involves evaluating a client's current fitness level, including things like strength, flexibility, and cardiovascular endurance. The trainer may use tools like body fat measurements, heart rate monitors, and strength tests to get a clear picture of the client's baseline fitness.

- Developing personalized exercise plans: Based on the client's goals and fitness level, the trainer will create a customized exercise plan that is designed to help them achieve their desired results. This might include specific exercises, cardio routines, and dietary recommendations.

- Demonstrating proper exercise techniques: A key part of a personal trainer's job is to teach their clients how to perform exercises safely and effectively. This involves providing demonstrations, correcting form, and offering feedback to ensure that the client is performing each movement correctly.

- Monitoring progress: Over time, the trainer will track the client's progress, assessing changes in strength, body composition, and overall fitness. This helps them adjust the exercise plan as necessary and provide ongoing support and motivation.

Becoming a personal trainer requires a combination of education and experience. Many trainers have a degree in exercise science, kinesiology, or a related field, and they may also hold certifications from organizations like the National Academy of Sports Medicine (NASM) or the American Council on Exercise (ACE).

PETROLEUM ENGINEER

Petroleum engineering is a fascinating field that deals with the exploration, production, and refinement of oil and gas resources. Petroleum engineers play a critical role in developing the technology and strategies necessary to extract and process these resources in the most efficient and cost-effective ways possible. Here's a closer look at what a petroleum engineer does.

Petroleum engineers work in a variety of settings, from oil rigs and drilling sites to refineries and laboratories. Their job is to use their expertise in math, science, and engineering to identify, locate, and extract oil and gas reserves from the earth. They also help to design and develop new technologies for extracting and refining these resources.

One of the most important aspects of a petroleum engineer's job is to locate and evaluate potential oil and gas reserves. This involves using geological surveys and other data to determine the location, size, and quality of the reserves. They also study the geology and geography of the area to determine the best way to extract the resources.

Once they have located the reserves, petroleum engineers work on designing and developing the methods and technologies necessary to extract the oil and gas. This includes designing and building drilling equipment and techniques, and developing processes for separating the oil and gas from other materials. They also work on developing new methods for processing and refining the resources, with an emphasis on minimizing waste and maximizing efficiency.

Petroleum engineers also play a critical role in monitoring the production and processing of oil and gas resources. This involves analyzing data and monitoring production levels to ensure that the resources are being extracted and processed in the most efficient way possible.

In addition to these technical duties, petroleum engineers also work closely with other professionals, including geologists, environmental scientists, and business executives. They provide technical expertise and advice, and help to develop and implement strategies for optimizing the production and profitability of the resources.

To become a petroleum engineer, you typically need at least a bachelor's degree in petroleum engineering or a related field. Many petroleum engineers also have advanced degrees, such as a master's or a Ph.D. in petroleum engineering or a related field. In addition to formal education, petroleum engineers also need a strong understanding of math, science, and engineering principles, as well as excellent problem-solving skills and the ability to work well in a team environment.

PHARMACIST

Pharmacists are healthcare professionals who are responsible for dispensing medications to patients. They play a critical role in ensuring that patients receive the right medications in the right doses, as well as providing education and counseling about drug interactions, side effects, and other important information.

Pharmacists work in a variety of settings, including community pharmacies, hospitals, long-term care facilities, and research labs. They may also work for government agencies, pharmaceutical companies, or health insurance companies.

One of the primary responsibilities of a pharmacist is to ensure that patients receive the correct medication and dosage prescribed by their healthcare provider. Pharmacists must have a thorough understanding of drug interactions, as well as potential side effects and adverse reactions. They must also be able to interpret and evaluate prescription orders to ensure that they are accurate and appropriate for the patient.

In addition to dispensing medications, pharmacists are also responsible for counseling patients on the proper use of their medications. This includes information on how to take the medication, potential side effects, and what to do if the patient misses a dose or experiences an adverse reaction. Pharmacists may also provide advice on over-the-counter medications, supplements, and home remedies.

Another important aspect of a pharmacist's job is to ensure that the medications they dispense are stored properly and have not expired. Pharmacists must also keep detailed records of all medications dispensed, as well as maintain up-to-date patient profiles to ensure that drug interactions or allergies are avoided.

Pharmacists also play a critical role in public health, especially in the current global pandemic. Many pharmacies have become vaccination sites, and pharmacists are administering COVID-19 vaccines to patients. They also provide education on how to protect ourselves from the virus.

Pharmacists must have a strong scientific background and a deep understanding of chemistry and biology. They must also have excellent communication and interpersonal skills, as they often work closely with patients and other healthcare professionals.

In addition to dispensing medications and providing patient education, pharmacists also have the opportunity to conduct research and contribute to the development of new medications. They may work in research institutions to conduct studies on the safety and efficacy of drugs or to develop new treatments for various health conditions.

PHOTOGRAPHER

Photographers are professionals who specialize in taking photographs, whether it's for personal or commercial use. They use cameras to capture images of people, landscapes, events, products, or anything else that can be photographed. Photographers use a variety of techniques, equipment, and software to create images that are beautiful, impactful, and meaningful.

Photography is an art form, and photographers use their creativity and imagination to tell stories, evoke emotions, and capture the essence of their subjects. They may use different techniques to create different effects, such as lighting, filters, or lenses. Photographers also need to have excellent technical skills, including understanding of exposure, composition, and editing software.

There are many different types of photographers, each specializing in a different area. For example, wedding photographers take pictures of weddings and other special events, while commercial photographers create images for advertising and marketing campaigns. Portrait photographers capture images of people, and sports photographers focus on capturing action and movement in sporting events.

One of the most important skills for a photographer is the ability to communicate with their subjects. Photographers need to be able to put their subjects at ease and make them feel comfortable in front of the camera. They also need to be able to direct their subjects and give them instructions on how to pose or where to stand to get the best shot.

Another important aspect of photography is post-processing. After the photos are taken, photographers need to edit them to improve their quality or add special effects. They use a variety of software tools to crop, adjust lighting and color, and remove imperfections. Post-processing is often just as important as taking the photo, as it can dramatically enhance the final product.

Photographers may work for themselves or for a company, depending on their specialty. Some photographers work on a freelance basis and are hired by clients for specific projects, while others work for a specific company or publication. Photographers need to be able to manage their time and workload effectively, as they may have multiple projects and deadlines to juggle at once.

If you're interested in becoming a photographer, it's important to practice your skills and develop your portfolio. You can start by taking pictures of your family and friends, and then progress to more complex projects. There are also many photography courses and workshops available that can help you improve your skills and learn new techniques.

PHYSICAL THERAPIST

Physical therapy is a field that helps people recover from injuries or illnesses that affect their ability to move and function properly. Physical therapists are healthcare professionals who work with patients to improve their mobility, relieve pain, and restore physical function.

A physical therapist's job involves a lot of different tasks. First, they must evaluate a patient's condition and develop a treatment plan. They work with patients to identify their goals and determine what they need to do to achieve them. This may include exercises, stretches, and other physical therapies.

Once a treatment plan is developed, physical therapists work with their patients to implement it. This may involve teaching patients how to perform specific exercises or stretches, providing manual therapy, or using specialized equipment to help patients improve their strength, flexibility, and range of motion.

Physical therapists also work closely with other healthcare professionals, such as doctors, nurses, and occupational therapists. They may consult with these professionals to develop a more comprehensive treatment plan that addresses all aspects of a patient's health.

In addition to working with patients, physical therapists must also keep detailed records of their treatments and progress. This helps them monitor their patients' progress and adjust their treatment plans as needed.

Physical therapists may work in a variety of settings, including hospitals, clinics, private practices, and nursing homes. They may also work with athletes to help them recover from sports-related injuries.

To become a physical therapist, you will typically need to earn a Doctor of Physical Therapy (DPT) degree. This requires completing a graduate-level program that includes coursework in anatomy, physiology, biomechanics, and other related fields. You will also need to complete a clinical internship or residency to gain hands-on experience working with patients.

In summary, physical therapists play an important role in helping people recover from injuries and illnesses that affect their ability to move and function properly. They work closely with patients to develop and implement individualized treatment plans that help them achieve their goals and regain their mobility and independence. If you enjoy helping others and are interested in healthcare, physical therapy may be an exciting and rewarding career path to consider.

PHYSICIAN ASSISTANT

Physician assistants (PAs) are healthcare professionals who work in collaboration with physicians and other members of the healthcare team to provide medical care. They are trained to diagnose and treat a wide range of medical conditions, and they are often the primary care provider for patients. PAs work in a variety of settings, including hospitals, clinics, and private practices.

One of the primary roles of a PA is to take medical histories and perform physical exams on patients. They use this information to make a diagnosis, develop a treatment plan, and prescribe medication when necessary. PAs also order and interpret diagnostic tests, such as X-rays and blood tests, to help diagnose and monitor medical conditions.

Another important role of PAs is to provide patient education. They help patients understand their medical conditions and treatments, and they teach them how to manage their health at home. PAs also help patients navigate the healthcare system, including scheduling appointments with specialists and coordinating care with other members of the healthcare team.

In addition to providing direct patient care, PAs may also perform a variety of administrative tasks. They may help with billing and coding, manage patient records, and help with other administrative tasks as needed. PAs may also be involved in quality improvement initiatives, such as developing and implementing clinical guidelines to improve patient outcomes.

To become a PA, one must complete a master's degree program in physician assistant studies. These programs typically take two years to complete and include both classroom and clinical training. Upon graduation, PAs must pass a national certification exam and obtain a state license to practice.

One of the great things about being a PA is the variety of settings in which they can work. PAs can specialize in a particular area of medicine, such as cardiology, pediatrics, or emergency medicine. They can also work in a variety of settings, including hospitals, clinics, private practices, and even in rural or underserved areas.

Overall, PAs play a vital role in the healthcare system. They work closely with physicians and other members of the healthcare team to provide high-quality medical care to patients. PAs must be skilled in both medical knowledge and interpersonal communication to provide the best possible care to patients. If you're interested in a career in healthcare, becoming a physician assistant could be a great option!

PHYSICIST

A physicist is a scientist who studies the fundamental laws of nature and the properties of matter and energy. Physicists are interested in understanding the underlying principles that govern the behavior of the universe at both the macroscopic and microscopic scales.

At its core, physics is the study of matter and energy and how they interact with each other. Physicists aim to develop theories and models that can explain and predict the behavior of physical systems. They use mathematics, experimentation, and computational simulations to test these theories and models, and to develop new insights into the nature of the universe.

Physicists work in a variety of areas, including astrophysics, condensed matter physics, particle physics, and biophysics. Astrophysicists study the behavior and properties of stars, galaxies, and other celestial bodies, while condensed matter physicists investigate the properties of solids and liquids. Particle physicists study the fundamental particles and forces that make up the universe, while biophysicists use the tools of physics to study biological systems.

One of the most famous examples of a physicist is Albert Einstein, who is known for his theories of special and general relativity, which transformed our understanding of space and time. But physicists are involved in a wide range of important scientific endeavors, from the development of new technologies to the study of the most fundamental questions about the universe.

Physicists work in a variety of settings, including universities, government labs, and private industry. They may conduct experiments, design new instruments and technologies, or analyze data from existing experiments and observations. They also collaborate with other scientists and engineers to solve complex problems and to develop new technologies.

In addition to conducting research, physicists also play an important role in education and outreach. They may teach courses in physics, mentor students and other scientists, or participate in public lectures and other outreach events. They may also work with policymakers to inform decisions related to science and technology.

Becoming a physicist requires a strong foundation in math and science. Most physicists hold advanced degrees, such as a Ph.D., and have completed specialized training in a particular field of physics. They must be skilled at designing and conducting experiments, analyzing data, and communicating their findings to others.

PLUMBER

Becoming a plumber means diving into an exciting world of hands-on work, where you tackle a variety of tasks that keep essential water and waste systems running smoothly. As a plumber, you'll be fixing issues that people rely on daily. With a constant demand for skilled plumbers, you can expect a stable and rewarding career.

To kick off your plumbing journey, you'll need training and hands-on experience through vocational courses, apprenticeships, or both. Trade schools and community colleges offer engaging plumbing courses that teach essential skills, such as reading blueprints, working with various pipe materials, and understanding plumbing codes. Finishing a program prepares you to enter the plumbing world confidently.

Apprenticeships provide a fantastic opportunity to learn plumbing while earning money. Lasting 4-5 years, these programs combine on-the-job training with classroom learning. You'll work on real plumbing tasks, such as:

1. Installing and repairing pipes that carry water, gas, or sewage.

2. Fixing or replacing faulty fixtures like faucets, toilets, and showerheads.

3. Clearing clogged drains and pipes using specialized tools and techniques.

4. Installing and maintaining water heaters and boilers.

5. Working with advanced plumbing systems, such as those in commercial buildings

6. Collaborating with architects and builders on the layout of plumbing systems.

After mastering the trade, you'll need a license to show your professional expertise. Passing an exam that tests your knowledge of plumbing codes, best practices, and safety will earn you that license, boosting your credibility and job opportunities.

As a licensed plumber, you can work in various settings, including plumbing companies, construction sites, or maintenance departments. You might even start your own business and find clients. With experience, you could explore specialized areas like pipefitting, steamfitting, or sprinkler system installation.

In summary, becoming a plumber is an exciting adventure full of hands-on work, diverse opportunities, and the chance to make a positive impact on people's lives. If you enjoy working with your hands, solving real-world problems, and being an essential part of society, a career as a plumber offers a fun, rewarding, and fascinating experience.

POLICE OFFICER

A police officer is someone who is responsible for keeping the public safe and maintaining law and order in their community. They work in partnership with their fellow officers and the local community to prevent crime, investigate offenses, and catch criminals.

Police officers are trained in a wide variety of skills, from communication and community relations to self-defense and emergency response. They must be able to remain calm and level-headed in high-pressure situations, such as emergencies or confrontations with violent individuals.

One of the most important parts of a police officer's job is to patrol the community, whether by foot, bicycle, or vehicle, to monitor activity and ensure that everyone is safe. They may also be called upon to respond to calls for service, such as reports of domestic disturbances, thefts, or accidents.

When a crime occurs, a police officer is often one of the first on the scene to investigate. They must be able to gather and evaluate evidence, interview witnesses, and piece together what happened in order to apprehend the suspect. They work with a team of detectives and other law enforcement professionals to ensure that the perpetrator is caught and brought to justice.

In addition to their work on the streets, police officers also perform administrative duties, such as preparing reports, maintaining records, and updating crime databases. They must be able to communicate effectively with other officers and the public, and be comfortable using a range of technology and software programs.

To become a police officer, individuals must first complete training at a police academy. This typically involves several months of intense physical and mental preparation, where they learn everything from defensive tactics to firearms training to constitutional law. They may also be required to pass various physical and written tests to demonstrate their abilities.

Overall, being a police officer can be a very rewarding career for those who are passionate about helping others and keeping their community safe. While it can be a challenging and dangerous job at times, it offers the opportunity to make a positive impact on the lives of others and to serve as a role model for future generations.

PRIVATE BANKER

A private banker is a professional who provides banking and financial services to wealthy individuals or high net worth clients. This can include managing their financial portfolios, advising on investments, and helping clients to make strategic decisions about their financial goals. Private bankers work in a highly specialized field, where they must have extensive knowledge of financial markets, investment strategies, and the specific needs of wealthy clients.

One of the main responsibilities of a private banker is to develop and manage relationships with clients. This means taking a highly personalized approach to their clients, learning their financial goals and objectives, and helping them to develop a customized investment strategy that aligns with their unique needs. Private bankers need to be skilled at building relationships and have excellent communication skills, as they will be working with clients who have very specific financial goals and expectations.

Private bankers also need to have a deep understanding of financial markets and investment strategies. They must stay up to date on market trends and be able to provide timely and accurate advice to their clients. This requires an in-depth understanding of financial instruments, such as stocks, bonds, and derivatives, as well as knowledge of economic indicators and other factors that can influence investment decisions.

One of the most important aspects of a private banker's role is risk management. Clients entrust private bankers with their wealth, and it is the private banker's job to ensure that those investments are protected from market volatility and other risks. This means developing a risk management strategy that is tailored to each client's individual needs, and regularly monitoring the performance of their investments to ensure they are on track to meet their goals.

In addition to working with clients, private bankers also work closely with other professionals in the financial services industry. This can include investment managers, wealth advisors, and tax experts. Private bankers need to be able to collaborate with these professionals to develop comprehensive financial plans that are tailored to their clients' unique needs.

To become a private banker, you typically need a bachelor's degree in finance, economics, or a related field, although some private banks may require a master's degree. One of the benefits of working as a private banker is the potential for a lucrative career. Private bankers typically earn a base salary, as well as commissions and bonuses based on the performance of their clients' investments.

PRIVATE INVESTIGATOR

Becoming a private investigator means stepping into a world of mystery and intrigue, where you'll use your sharp mind and keen observation skills to solve cases and uncover hidden truths. As a private investigator, you'll work on a wide range of assignments, from tracking down missing persons to uncovering corporate fraud. Your work will not only be thrilling but also essential in bringing justice and closure to those in need.

To begin your journey as a private investigator, you'll need a solid foundation in investigation techniques and relevant laws. Many community colleges and online platforms offer courses in criminal justice, surveillance, and research methods. Gaining knowledge in these areas will prepare you for the challenges and excitement of the private investigation world.

While formal education is essential, hands-on experience is invaluable for private investigators. Consider working alongside seasoned professionals or seeking internships at investigation agencies to gain real-world experience. You'll have the chance to work on cases such as:

1. Locating missing persons or tracking down fugitives.

2. Conducting background checks and pre-employment screenings.

3. Investigating insurance fraud, corporate espionage, or intellectual property theft.

4. Gathering evidence for legal cases, such as divorce or child custody disputes.

5. Conducting surveillance on persons of interest.

6. Researching and analyzing information to uncover hidden details or connections.

As a private investigator, you'll have diverse employment opportunities. You can work for investigation agencies, law firms, or even start your own business. You might also specialize in niche areas like cybersecurity, financial fraud, or personal protection.

In summary, becoming a private investigator is an exciting journey full of mystery, and challenges. You'll tackle various assignments, from tracking down missing persons to uncovering hidden secrets. If you're fascinated by the world of investigation, have a knack for problem-solving, and are driven by a desire to help others, a career as a private investigator promises a thrilling, rewarding, and captivating experience.

PRODUCT DESIGNER

A product designer is someone who is responsible for creating new and innovative products. They work to develop products that people will want to use and enjoy. These products can range from everyday household items to electronic devices and even furniture. Product designers are creative problem solvers who take into account the needs and desires of users, the materials and production methods available, and the overall aesthetic of the design.

To be a successful product designer, one must have a strong sense of creativity and design, as well as a keen eye for detail. The designer must be able to envision how the product will be used and how it will fit into the lives of its users. They must also have a deep understanding of the materials and manufacturing processes involved in bringing a product from concept to reality.

The process of designing a product can be broken down into several stages. First, the designer must research the market and identify a need for a new product or an improvement on an existing one. They will then create a concept, which is a rough outline of what the product will look like and how it will function. This is usually done in the form of sketches or 3D models.

Next, the designer will create detailed specifications for the product. This includes choosing the appropriate materials, creating engineering drawings, and working out the production process. They may also need to create a prototype of the product to test its functionality and make any necessary adjustments.

Once the product design is finalized, the designer will work with manufacturers to produce the product on a larger scale. They may need to make adjustments to the design based on the capabilities of the manufacturing process or the availability of certain materials.

Product designers work in a variety of industries, from consumer goods to medical equipment. They may work for large companies or as independent consultants. Some designers may specialize in a particular type of product, such as toys or furniture, while others may work on a wide range of products.

In conclusion, product designers are creative problem solvers who play a crucial role in the creation of new and innovative products. They must have a strong sense of creativity and design, a deep understanding of materials and manufacturing processes, and the ability to work with a wide range of people. Being a product designer is an exciting and rewarding career that can have a significant impact on people's lives.

PRODUCT MANAGER

A product manager is a professional responsible for developing and executing the strategy for a company's product or product line. This involves working closely with a team of engineers, designers, marketers, and other stakeholders to create and refine the product from its conception to its launch and beyond.

Product managers are responsible for conducting market research, identifying customer needs and problems, and creating a product roadmap that outlines the product's features, functionality, and design. They work closely with cross-functional teams to ensure that the product meets the needs of the customer and is delivered on time and within budget.

In addition to developing the product, a product manager is also responsible for creating and executing the product's go-to-market strategy. This involves identifying the target market, creating marketing and sales plans, and working with the sales team to ensure the product is effectively promoted and sold to customers. Product managers also work with customer support and operations teams to ensure that the product is delivered and supported properly.

One of the key roles of a product manager is to be a liaison between various teams within a company. They must work closely with the engineering team to ensure that the product is built according to the specifications, with the marketing team to ensure that the product is effectively promoted, and with the sales team to ensure that the product is being sold properly. They also work closely with upper management to ensure that the product is meeting company goals and objectives.

Product managers must have strong communication and leadership skills, as they must lead cross-functional teams and work with stakeholders at all levels of the company. They must also be strategic thinkers who can balance short-term and long-term goals, and must be able to make data-driven decisions based on market research and customer feedback.

Overall, a product manager is a strategic leader who is responsible for the entire lifecycle of a product, from its conception to its launch and beyond. They must work closely with cross-functional teams, have strong communication and leadership skills, and be adaptable and able to work in a fast-paced environment. A product manager is critical to the success of a product and is a key player in the company's overall success.

PROFESSIONAL ATHLETE

Professional athletes are highly skilled individuals who have dedicated their lives to the pursuit of physical excellence in their chosen sport. They are driven by a love of competition, a desire to win, and a passion for pushing themselves to their limits.

At the highest level of competition, professional athletes are the best in the world in their respective disciplines. They train tirelessly, day after day, to develop the strength, speed, agility, and coordination necessary to perform at the highest level. They work with coaches, trainers, and other support staff to develop and refine their skills, and they are constantly looking for ways to improve and stay ahead of the competition.

Professional athletes come from all walks of life and compete in a wide variety of sports, from football, basketball, and baseball to golf, tennis, and gymnastics. Some athletes compete individually, while others are part of a team, but all share a dedication to their sport and a relentless pursuit of excellence.

One of the most challenging aspects of being a professional athlete is the intense physical demands of the job. Athletes must be in peak physical condition in order to compete at the highest level, and they must be able to withstand the physical toll that their sport takes on their bodies. This requires not only physical training, but also a commitment to a healthy diet, adequate rest and recovery, and other lifestyle factors that can help athletes maintain their physical and mental health.

In addition to the physical demands of the job, professional athletes also face a unique set of mental challenges. They must learn to manage the pressure of competition, deal with the stress of intense training and competition schedules, and maintain a positive attitude and mental focus even in the face of setbacks and challenges.

Despite the challenges, many professional athletes find the rewards of their work to be incredibly fulfilling. They get to travel the world, meet new people, and compete at the highest levels of their sport. They also have the opportunity to inspire others and serve as role models for aspiring athletes and sports fans around the world.

In order to become a professional athlete, individuals must typically start training at a young age and commit themselves to years of hard work, discipline, and dedication.

At the professional level, athletes are typically paid for their performance and may also receive endorsements, sponsorships, and other opportunities to earn income related to their sport. They may also work with agents and other representatives to negotiate contracts, manage their finances, and build their personal brands.

PROJECT MANAGER

Project managers are the masterminds behind the successful completion of projects. They are responsible for ensuring that a project is delivered on time, within budget, and to the satisfaction of the client. A project manager's role is to take the lead on the planning, implementation, monitoring, and closure of a project. They are the glue that holds the team together and ensures everyone is working towards the same goal.

As a project manager, you would be responsible for a wide range of tasks. These might include defining the project's scope, developing a project plan, setting milestones and timelines, managing budgets, identifying and managing risks, managing project resources, and providing regular progress reports to stakeholders. You would also be responsible for managing the project team, ensuring everyone has the resources they need to do their jobs, and managing any conflicts that may arise.

One of the most interesting things about being a project manager is that you get to work on a wide variety of projects. Projects can vary in size, scope, and complexity, and can be found in a wide range of industries. You might work on a construction project one day, a marketing campaign the next, and a software development project the day after that. This variety means that you are constantly learning new things, meeting new people, and facing new challenges.

Another interesting aspect of being a project manager is that you get to work with people from different areas of the organization. You might work with people from finance, marketing, sales, engineering, or operations, depending on the project you are working on. This means that you get to learn about different parts of the business, and how they all fit together. You also get to build relationships with people across the organization, which can be very rewarding.

To be a successful project manager, you need to be a great communicator. You need to be able to explain the project's goals and objectives to stakeholders, communicate with team members, and manage any conflicts that may arise. You also need to be a great listener, as you need to be able to take on board feedback from stakeholders and team members, and use this to improve the project.

Overall, being a project manager can be a very rewarding career. You get to work on a variety of projects, learn new things, and work with people from across the organization. If you are organized, have great communication skills, and love the idea of managing a project from start to finish, then project management may be the perfect career for you.

PROPERTY MANAGER

Property managers are responsible for overseeing the day-to-day operations of various types of real estate properties. This includes residential properties such as apartment buildings, condominiums, and townhouses, as well as commercial properties such as office buildings, retail spaces, and industrial warehouses. They work closely with property owners to ensure that their properties are well-maintained and profitable.

One of the key roles of a property manager is to act as a liaison between the owner of the property and the tenants or renters. They are responsible for finding new tenants, negotiating leases, and collecting rent payments. They are also responsible for ensuring that tenants follow the terms of the lease agreement and for taking legal action against tenants who do not comply.

In addition to finding new tenants and collecting rent, property managers are also responsible for maintaining the physical condition of the property. This includes coordinating repairs and maintenance services, conducting inspections of the property, and ensuring that the property is in compliance with all local and state regulations.

Another important role of property managers is to handle all financial aspects of the property. This includes creating and managing a budget for the property, handling financial transactions such as rent payments and security deposits, and keeping detailed records of all financial transactions related to the property.

Property managers also have a responsibility to maintain a positive relationship with the tenants and the surrounding community. They are often the first point of contact for tenants who have concerns or complaints, and it is their responsibility to address these concerns and ensure that tenants are satisfied with their living or working environment. Additionally, property managers may work with local government officials to address any concerns or issues that arise in the surrounding community.

To be a successful property manager, one must have a strong knowledge of real estate law and regulations, as well as excellent communication and interpersonal skills. They must be able to manage multiple tasks at once, work well under pressure, and be able to problem-solve effectively.

In conclusion, property managers play an important role in the real estate industry. They are responsible for ensuring that properties are well-maintained and profitable, that tenants are satisfied, and that the property is in compliance with all local and state regulations. Property management can be a challenging and rewarding career for those who are passionate about real estate and are able to work well under pressure.

PSYCHIATRIST

Psychiatrists are doctors who specialize in the study, diagnosis, and treatment of mental illness. They are trained to understand how the brain and the body work together, and they use this knowledge to help people who are struggling with emotional and behavioral problems.

One of the main things that a psychiatrist does is diagnose mental illnesses. They use a combination of observation, conversation, and medical tests to figure out what is causing a person's symptoms. This is important because it helps the psychiatrist determine the best course of treatment for their patient.

Psychiatrists use a wide range of treatments to help their patients, and these treatments can be different depending on the patient's individual needs. One of the most common treatments is therapy. This can involve talking one-on-one with the psychiatrist, or it can involve group therapy or family therapy. Therapy can help people work through their emotional problems and develop better coping skills.

In addition to therapy, psychiatrists also prescribe medications to help their patients manage their symptoms. These can include antidepressants, anti-anxiety medications, and mood stabilizers. The psychiatrist will work closely with their patient to determine the right medication and dosage for their needs, and will also monitor their patient's progress and adjust the medication as needed.

Another important part of a psychiatrist's job is to educate their patients about mental illness. They help their patients understand their condition, what causes it, and how they can manage it. This can involve teaching patients coping skills, stress reduction techniques, and other strategies for dealing with the challenges of mental illness.

Psychiatrists work in a variety of settings, including hospitals, clinics, private practices, and government agencies. They often work closely with other healthcare professionals, including psychologists, social workers, and nurses, to ensure that their patients receive comprehensive and effective care.

Overall, psychiatrists play an important role in helping people with mental illness. By providing diagnosis, treatment, and education, they help their patients manage their symptoms and improve their quality of life. If you are interested in becoming a psychiatrist, you will need to complete medical school and specialized training in psychiatry, as well as be dedicated to helping people in need.

PSYCHOLOGIST

The career path of a psychologist leads you into a fascinating world where you'll explore the complexities of the human mind and help people improve their mental health and well-being. As a psychologist, you'll dig into the mysteries of human behavior, emotions, and cognition, applying your knowledge to make a positive impact on individuals.

To begin your journey as a psychologist, you'll need to pursue higher education, starting with a bachelor's degree in psychology or a related field. During your undergraduate studies, you'll be exposed to intriguing topics such as cognitive psychology, developmental psychology, and social psychology. This strong foundation will prepare you for the exciting world of psychological research and practice.

Licensing requirements for psychologists vary by region, but typically involve completing a doctoral program, gaining supervised experience, and passing a licensing examination. Obtaining a license will demonstrate your competence and commitment to ethical practice, boosting your credibility and leading to career opportunities.

As a psychologist, you'll have diverse and rewarding work options, such as:

1. Providing therapy to individuals, couples, or families facing emotional or behavioral challenges.

2. Assessing and diagnosing mental health disorders and developing treatment plans.

3. Working in schools or universities, supporting students' mental health and academic success.

4. Assisting organizations in improving employee well-being.

5. Conducting research to advance the understanding of human behavior and mental processes.

6. Teaching and training future generations of psychologists.

To remain current in the ever-evolving field of psychology, it's essential to engage in lifelong learning. Attend conferences, workshops, and seminars to stay informed about the latest theories, techniques, and research findings. This commitment to professional development will help you maintain your expertise and adapt to the changing needs of the clients and communities you serve.

PUBLIC RELATIONS SPECIALIST

Public Relations (PR) Specialists play a vital role in helping organizations and individuals manage their image and reputation. PR Specialists use a variety of techniques to communicate and create a positive public image for their clients, including media relations, social media, special events, and crisis management.

One of the primary responsibilities of a PR Specialist is to establish and maintain relationships with media outlets. They write press releases and pitch stories to journalists in an effort to get positive media coverage for their clients. PR Specialists need to have excellent writing and communication skills to be effective in their job. They also need to be able to think creatively to come up with new and innovative ways to promote their clients and their products or services.

In addition to media relations, PR Specialists also manage their clients' social media presence. Social media has become an increasingly important tool for PR Specialists to reach a wider audience and engage with customers in a more personal way. They create content for social media platforms, such as Facebook, Twitter, and Instagram, and monitor their clients' online reputation.

Another important role of a PR Specialist is event planning. They organize and manage events such as press conferences, product launches, and charity events. These events are an excellent way to generate publicity for their clients and to create a positive image for them in the community. PR Specialists need to have excellent organizational skills and be able to work well under pressure to plan and execute successful events.

Crisis management is another important aspect of a PR Specialist's job. When a crisis occurs, such as a product recall or a negative news story, a PR Specialist is responsible for managing the situation and mitigating the damage to their client's reputation. They work with the media to provide accurate and timely information, and they develop strategies to help their clients recover from the crisis.

To be a successful PR Specialist, one must possess a range of skills and qualities. These include excellent communication skills, both written and verbal, creativity, strategic thinking, and the ability to work well under pressure. PR Specialists also need to be able to work collaboratively with clients, media contacts, and other stakeholders. They must be adaptable and able to quickly adjust to changing circumstances, such as the emergence of a crisis situation.

RACE DRIVER

A race driver is a highly skilled and trained professional who competes in a variety of high-speed motorsports events, such as Formula One, NASCAR, IndyCar, Rally, and many others. These drivers are responsible for racing highly complex, high-performance vehicles on a wide range of tracks, often in extreme and challenging conditions.

At its core, the role of a race driver is to maneuver their car or vehicle around a designated course or track as quickly as possible. This requires an exceptional level of physical fitness, mental focus, and technical skill, as well as a deep understanding of the mechanics of their vehicle, its limitations, and its potential.

Race drivers can compete in a variety of different events, each with its unique challenges and requirements. For example, in Formula One racing, drivers must be able to handle the immense G-forces that are generated by high-speed cornering, while in NASCAR and other oval-track events, drivers must be able to maintain a precise line around a banked circuit while jockeying for position with other drivers. In rally racing, drivers must contend with changing terrain, weather conditions, and other obstacles, while in endurance racing, they must be able to maintain consistent, high-speed driving over long periods, often in grueling weather conditions.

Regardless of the type of event or race they are competing in, race drivers must possess a high level of technical skill and knowledge, as well as an understanding of how to read and respond to their environment. This means being able to analyze and adjust to changes in track conditions, weather, and other factors, while maintaining a high level of precision and control over their vehicle.

Beyond their physical and technical skills, race drivers must also possess a strong competitive drive and an unwavering focus on achieving their goals. This requires mental resilience, the ability to perform under pressure, and a deep understanding of the intricacies of their chosen sport.

In addition to the skills required to compete successfully, race drivers must also be able to manage and market themselves effectively. This involves building relationships with sponsors, managing their finances, and developing a personal brand that can help them stand out in an increasingly competitive field.

Ultimately, the life of a race driver requires a relentless drive to improve, an untiring commitment to success, and a deep passion for the sport of high-speed racing. While the job can be physically and emotionally demanding, for those who are able to succeed, the rewards can be tremendous, including fame, and fortune.

REAL ESTATE AGENT

A real estate agent is a licensed professional who helps people buy, sell, or rent properties. They act as a mediator between buyers and sellers or landlords and tenants, working to ensure that both parties are satisfied with the transaction.

Real estate agents are experts in the local housing market, and they use their knowledge to help their clients make informed decisions. They research market trends, property values, and zoning laws to help buyers find the right property at the best possible price. They also help sellers set a fair price for their property and market it to potential buyers.

To become a real estate agent, one must first obtain a license. This typically requires completing a certain number of hours of pre-licensing coursework, passing a licensing exam, and meeting other state requirements. Once licensed, real estate agents can work independently or with a brokerage firm.

One of the key roles of a real estate agent is to provide guidance and support throughout the entire buying or selling process. They help their clients understand complex real estate contracts, negotiate deals, and coordinate with other professionals such as attorneys and home inspectors. They also handle all the paperwork and legal requirements involved in a transaction.

In addition to helping clients buy and sell properties, real estate agents also assist with property management. They help landlords find tenants, screen potential renters, and handle lease agreements. They also act as a point of contact for tenants, handling maintenance requests and other issues as they arise.

To be successful as a real estate agent, one must possess a range of skills. Strong communication skills are essential, as agents must be able to clearly and effectively communicate with clients, colleagues, and other professionals. They must also be good problem-solvers, able to think creatively and find solutions to complex issues.

Real estate agents must also be skilled negotiators, able to navigate the often-complicated process of buying or selling a property. They must be detail-oriented, with strong organizational skills to keep track of paperwork, deadlines, and other details.

Finally, successful real estate agents must be personable and able to build strong relationships with their clients. They must be able to understand their clients' needs and goals, and work to find the best possible solutions for them.

RENEWABLE ENERGY TECHNICIAN

Renewable energy technicians are professionals who install, maintain, and repair equipment used to harness renewable energy sources, such as wind, solar, hydro, and geothermal power. Their work is vital to the development of sustainable energy sources that reduce our reliance on fossil fuels and promote a cleaner environment.

The job of a renewable energy technician is diverse and involves a range of skills, including electrical and mechanical engineering, computer programming, and project management. They work in various settings, from power plants and wind farms to remote sites and homes. Their work is often done outdoors and requires physical fitness, as they often climb turbines, work on roofs, and carry heavy equipment.

One of the most important aspects of the renewable energy technician's job is to install, maintain and repair renewable energy systems. They start by evaluating a site's suitability for renewable energy and developing installation plans. Then they install the necessary equipment, which may include solar panels, wind turbines, and geothermal systems. They connect the systems to the power grid, and ensure that they meet all safety and environmental standards.

Another essential task of the renewable energy technician is to conduct regular maintenance on the installed systems. This may include cleaning solar panels, replacing worn-out parts, and inspecting and lubricating turbines. They also troubleshoot and repair any problems that may arise, whether due to technical or environmental issues.

Renewable energy technicians work with a variety of tools and equipment, including hand and power tools, diagnostic equipment, and computer software. They use these tools to test systems and components, monitor system performance, and make adjustments as necessary. They must also maintain accurate records of their work and communicate effectively with colleagues, customers, and supervisors.

In addition to installation and maintenance, renewable energy technicians also play a crucial role in research and development. They collaborate with engineers, scientists, and other professionals to test and develop new technologies that improve energy efficiency and harness renewable energy sources more effectively.

Renewable energy is a rapidly growing field, and there are many career opportunities for technicians with the right skills and qualifications. Some specialize in specific areas, such as solar energy or wind power, while others work in research and development or in the design and production of renewable energy systems.

RESTAURANT MANAGER

A restaurant manager is responsible for the day-to-day operations of a restaurant. They oversee the restaurant's staff, manage finances, and ensure customer satisfaction. This can be a challenging job that requires excellent leadership, communication, and organizational skills.

One of the primary responsibilities of a restaurant manager is to oversee the staff. They are responsible for hiring and training new employees, creating work schedules, and managing the restaurant's workflow. They must also ensure that employees are following proper health and safety guidelines, and that the restaurant is in compliance with laws.

In addition to managing the staff, restaurant managers must also manage the restaurant's finances. This includes tracking inventory, ordering supplies, and managing the restaurant's budget. They must also develop and implement pricing strategies to ensure that the restaurant is profitable.

Customer satisfaction is another important aspect of a restaurant manager's job. They are responsible for ensuring that customers are happy with their experience at the restaurant. This includes monitoring customer feedback and resolving any issues or complaints that arise. They must also ensure that the restaurant's atmosphere is welcoming and that the food and service meet the highest standards.

Restaurant managers must be skilled at multitasking and problem-solving. They must be able to handle a variety of issues that may arise during a shift, such as staffing shortages, equipment failures, or customer complaints. They must also be able to make quick decisions and communicate effectively with the restaurant's staff.

Another important aspect of the restaurant manager's job is marketing and promotion. They must develop marketing strategies to attract new customers and retain existing ones. This may include advertising in local publications, creating promotions or special offers, or using social media to promote the restaurant.

Restaurant managers may also be responsible for menu development and food preparation. They may work with the chef to create new dishes and ensure that the restaurant's food meets the highest standards of quality and taste. They may also be responsible for sourcing ingredients and ensuring that the restaurant is using the best possible suppliers.

In summary, a restaurant manager is a critical role in the hospitality industry. They are responsible for managing the staff, finances, and customer satisfaction of a restaurant.

ROBOTICS ENGINEER

A robotics engineer is a type of engineer who specializes in the design, development, and testing of robots. These professionals work with a range of robotic systems, from simple machines that perform basic tasks to complex robots that can perform multiple functions in different environments. The work of a robotics engineer is incredibly diverse and challenging, requiring a deep understanding of mechanical engineering, electrical engineering, and computer science.

The primary responsibility of a robotics engineer is to design, build, and test robots. This involves developing a clear understanding of the needs and requirements of the robot's intended application, as well as designing the mechanical components, electronic controls, and programming necessary to make the robot work. Robotics engineers must be able to analyze the tasks a robot will need to perform, and create designs that can accommodate those tasks.

One of the key skills of a robotics engineer is the ability to write computer code. Robots are essentially computerized machines, and the software that runs them is critical to their operation. Robotics engineers need to be proficient in programming languages such as C++, Python, and Java. They must be able to write and debug code, and work closely with other members of the development team to ensure the robot's software is reliable and efficient.

Robotics engineers must also have a strong foundation in electrical engineering, as the robots they design will require various sensors, motors, and other electronic components. They must be familiar with the various types of electrical circuits and have an understanding of power management and control systems.

In addition to their technical skills, robotics engineers must also be able to communicate effectively with others. They often work in teams with other engineers and technicians, as well as with clients or stakeholders who may not have a technical background. \

One of the most exciting aspects of working as a robotics engineer is the opportunity to work on cutting-edge technologies that are changing the world. Robotics is an emerging field that is driving innovation in industries ranging from manufacturing and transportation to healthcare and entertainment.

To become a robotics engineer, a degree in mechanical engineering, electrical engineering, or computer science is typically required. Many robotics engineers also have advanced degrees, such as a master's or doctorate in robotics or a related field.

ROCKET ENGINEER

Rocket engineering is a specialized field of engineering that focuses on the design, construction, and operation of rockets and other spacecraft. Rocket engineers use their knowledge of physics, mathematics, and other sciences to develop rockets that can take people and payloads to space and beyond.

One of the main roles of a rocket engineer is to design and test various rocket components, including engines, guidance systems, and other critical systems. These engineers must also make sure that the rocket can withstand the extreme conditions of launch and space travel, including high speeds, pressure, and temperature changes. They must also make sure that the rocket's trajectory is correct, and that it can safely land back on Earth if necessary.

Rocket engineers work closely with other professionals in the aerospace industry, including mechanical engineers, electrical engineers, and computer scientists. They collaborate to design and test different components, and they work together to make sure that the entire rocket is functioning correctly. For example, rocket engineers might work with mechanical engineers to design and test the rocket's structural components, or they might work with electrical engineers to develop and test the rocket's electrical systems.

Another important role of a rocket engineer is to ensure that the rocket is environmentally friendly. They must develop rockets that are both efficient and sustainable, and that do not harm the environment in any way. This means using clean and renewable energy sources, such as solar power, and developing new technologies that minimize waste and pollution.

Rocket engineers also play a critical role in space exploration. They design and build spacecraft that can explore other planets, moons, and asteroids. These spacecraft must be able to navigate long distances through space and operate in extremely harsh conditions. They must also be able to collect data and communicate with Earth from great distances.

To become a rocket engineer, a person typically needs a degree in aerospace engineering, mechanical engineering, or a related field. They must also have a strong understanding of physics, mathematics, and other sciences. Many rocket engineers go on to earn advanced degrees, such as a master's or doctorate, to further specialize in the field.

Rocket engineering is a challenging but rewarding career that offers the opportunity to work on cutting-edge technologies and push the boundaries of human knowledge and exploration. It requires a strong commitment to science, technology, and innovation, as well as a passion for space and exploration.

ROOFER

A roofer is a skilled tradesperson who specializes in the installation, repair, and maintenance of roofs on buildings. The primary function of a roof is to protect a building's interior and contents from the elements, including rain, snow, hail, wind, and sunlight. Roofers are responsible for ensuring that the roof is installed correctly and will perform its intended function effectively for as long as possible.

Roofers work on both residential and commercial buildings, and their job duties may vary depending on the type of building they are working on. For example, a roofer working on a residential building may be responsible for installing or repairing shingles, while a roofer working on a commercial building may work with materials like metal or flat roofing systems.

One of the key skills of a roofer is the ability to work at heights. Roofing work can be dangerous, as it often requires workers to climb up ladders or scaffolding to reach the roof. Roofers must take the proper safety precautions, such as wearing harnesses and using other protective equipment, to ensure that they remain safe while working at heights.

In addition to working at heights, roofers must also be physically fit and able to work in a variety of weather conditions. Roofing work is often done outside, so roofers must be able to work in hot, cold, or wet conditions as necessary. This can be physically demanding work, as it often involves lifting heavy materials and tools.

One of the primary job duties of a roofer is to install or repair roofs. This can involve measuring and cutting roofing materials to fit the specific dimensions of the roof, as well as installing materials like shingles, tiles, or metal roofing panels. Roofers must also ensure that the roof is properly sealed and waterproofed to prevent leaks.

In addition to their technical skills, roofers must also have good communication and customer service skills. They may need to communicate with clients to explain the work that needs to be done, answer any questions or concerns, and provide estimates for the cost of the job. They must also be able to work effectively as part of a team, often collaborating with other tradespeople like carpenters or electricians.

Finally, roofers must also stay up-to-date on the latest safety standards and regulations in the industry. They must be familiar with safety protocols for working at heights, as well as the use of safety equipment like harnesses and safety ropes. They must also be knowledgeable about building codes and regulations related to roofing work, to ensure that the work is done to the proper specifications.

SALES REPRESENTATIVE

Sales representatives play an important role in the world of business. Their job is to promote and sell products or services to customers, whether that be individuals, businesses, or organizations. Sales representatives use their communication and interpersonal skills to understand their customers' needs and wants, and then provide solutions that meet those needs.

The daily activities of a sales representative can vary widely depending on the product or service being sold and the industry they work in. For example, a sales representative selling software products may spend their time researching the needs of potential customers, identifying businesses that would benefit from the software, and reaching out to decision-makers within those companies to pitch their product. On the other hand, a sales representative selling consumer goods such as clothing or home appliances may spend more time working in retail stores, engaging with customers face-to-face to help them select products that meet their needs.

One of the key skills of a successful sales representative is the ability to build and maintain relationships with customers. This involves not only understanding their needs, but also being able to communicate effectively and build trust. Sales representatives often work with customers over a long period of time, so developing strong relationships is critical to building a loyal customer base.

Another important aspect of the job is staying up to date on industry trends and the competition. Sales representatives need to know what products or services their competitors are offering, what makes their own product or service unique, and how to differentiate themselves from other options in the market. They may attend trade shows or conferences to network with industry professionals, keep abreast of emerging trends and technologies, and build their personal brand.

Sales representatives may also work with marketing teams to create campaigns and promotions that help to generate interest in their product or service. This could involve developing targeted email campaigns, social media ads, or other marketing materials that help to spread the word about their offerings.

Sales representatives are often compensated through a combination of base salary and commission, so the potential for earning a high income is there for those who excel in the role. For many, the ability to work independently, develop relationships with customers, and have a direct impact on their company's success makes the job both challenging and rewarding.

SCIENTIST

Scientists are people who study the world around them in a systematic and organized way. They use experiments, observations, and data to uncover new knowledge and develop theories about how things work. Scientists are incredibly curious people who are always looking for answers to questions about the natural world, and they work in a wide range of fields, from physics and biology to astronomy and geology.

To become a scientist, you typically need to complete a formal education in a scientific field. This includes earning a Bachelor's degree in a related field, such as biology, chemistry, or physics, and often a Master's degree or PhD as well. Depending on the field of science, you may also need to obtain specific certifications or licenses to work in certain areas.

Once a scientist has completed their education and training, they can begin working in their field. Scientists typically work in research, conducting experiments and analyzing data to answer questions and develop new theories. They may work in academic settings, such as universities or research institutions, or in industry, such as pharmaceutical or biotech companies. Some scientists work in government agencies, such as the National Aeronautics and Space Administration (NASA) or the National Institutes of Health (NIH).

In their day-to-day work, scientists use a wide range of tools and techniques to conduct experiments and gather data. These may include microscopes, computers, specialized software, and various types of lab equipment. They may also use advanced technologies such as DNA sequencing, high-performance computing, or electron microscopy.

One of the most important aspects of being a scientist is the ability to communicate your findings to others. Scientists often publish their work in scientific journals, present at conferences and meetings, and speak to the media about their research.

In addition to conducting research and communicating their findings, scientists may also work on developing new technologies or products. For example, a chemist might work in a pharmaceutical company to develop new medicines, or an engineer might work to develop new materials for use in industry.

Finally, it's worth noting that being a scientist is not just about working in a lab or conducting experiments. Science is a way of thinking and approaching problems, and many scientists work in areas that are not traditionally thought of as "scientific." For example, social scientists may study human behavior or economics, while environmental scientists may study the impact of human activity on the natural world.

SCREENWRITER

A screenwriter is a writer who creates stories and scripts for television shows, movies, and other visual media. They are responsible for coming up with original ideas or adapting existing material, and crafting it into a story that can be effectively communicated through visual media.

Screenwriters must be able to create engaging and compelling stories that will resonate with their audience. This involves developing characters that the audience can identify with and care about, as well as a plot that will keep them engaged from beginning to end. Screenwriters must also be able to effectively convey their story through dialogue, creating lines that are not only realistic but also impactful and memorable.

The process of creating a script typically involves a great deal of research and planning. Before a screenwriter can begin writing, they must first come up with a story idea that is marketable and will appeal to a wide audience. Once they have their idea, they must develop it into a detailed plot, complete with well-developed characters and a clear structure.

From there, the screenwriter will begin to write the actual script. This can be a difficult and time-consuming process, as the writer must not only convey the story in a compelling way, but also ensure that the script adheres to specific formatting and industry standards.

In addition to writing the script, screenwriters may also be involved in the casting process and work with the director and producers to ensure that the vision for the story is realized on-screen. They may also work closely with actors to ensure that their lines are delivered in a way that effectively communicates the intended message.

Screenwriting is a highly competitive field, with many aspiring writers vying for a limited number of jobs. To succeed as a screenwriter, it is essential to have excellent writing skills, as well as a deep understanding of the film and television industry. Many successful screenwriters have also honed their craft through experience, either by working on their own projects or by working as an assistant to more established writers.

In addition to writing screenplays for movies and television shows, screenwriters may also write scripts for other visual media, such as video games or web series. They may also work as script doctors, helping to improve and refine scripts that have already been written.

SCULPTOR

Sculptors are artists who create three-dimensional works of art by carving, molding, casting, or assembling various materials such as stone, metal, wood, clay, or even found objects. Sculpture has been around for thousands of years and has played a significant role in human history and culture, with examples of ancient sculptures still existing today.

Sculptors often work independently, developing their own unique style and technique, but may also work as part of a team on larger projects. They create sculptures for various purposes, including public art installations, private commissions, and gallery exhibitions.

The process of creating a sculpture can take weeks, months, or even years, depending on the size and complexity of the piece. Sculptors may begin by creating sketches or models of their work before moving on to the final materials. Once they have a clear idea of what they want to create, they start the process of bringing their vision to life.

One common technique used by sculptors is carving. This involves removing material from a block or slab of stone, wood, or other material to create the desired shape. This can be done using chisels, hammers, and other tools. Some sculptors prefer to work with soft materials such as clay or wax, which can be easily molded and shaped. Others use metal or other materials that require casting, welding, or other specialized techniques.

Sculptors also need to have a good understanding of anatomy and form, as they often create sculptures of people or animals. They must be able to accurately represent the musculature and bone structure of the subject while also capturing its essence.

Sculptors must also have strong problem-solving skills. They need to be able to overcome challenges such as material limitations, structural issues, and technical difficulties in order to create their desired vision. They must be willing to experiment with new techniques and materials in order to push the boundaries of what is possible in sculpture.

Once a sculpture is complete, the sculptor must decide on the best way to display and exhibit their work. Some sculptures are intended to be displayed in public spaces, such as parks or museums, while others are designed for private collections or exhibitions. Sculptors may work with curators or gallery owners to promote and sell their work.

In addition to technical and creative skills, sculptors must also possess a strong work ethic and the ability to work independently. They often work long hours in solitude, focusing intensely on their work for extended periods of time. This requires a great deal of discipline and dedication to the craft.

SHIP CAPTAIN

A ship captain, also known as a skipper, commands the safe and efficient operation of a vessel, whether it be a cargo ship, tanker, cruise ship, or other type of watercraft. A ship captain must have a thorough knowledge of the ship, its capabilities, and the shipping industry as a whole. They must also be able to make quick decisions, manage a team of crew members, and ensure the safety of everyone on board.

The ship captain's main duties involve navigation, communication, and management. Navigation is the primary responsibility of the ship captain, who must plan the vessel's route, taking into account weather conditions, sea currents, and other factors that may impact the ship's journey. They also need to be familiar with the operation of the ship's navigation equipment, such as radar, GPS, and electronic charts. In addition to plotting the ship's course, they must also ensure that all crew members are aware of the route and any potential hazards.

Communication is another crucial responsibility of the ship captain. They are responsible for keeping the crew informed of any changes to the ship's course or schedule, as well as communicating with other ships, ports, and shipping companies. They must also be able to communicate effectively with crew members, ensuring that they understand their roles and responsibilities and that they are following all safety protocols.

In terms of management, the ship captain is responsible for overseeing the entire crew, which can range from a small team on a tugboat to hundreds of crew members on a large cruise ship. They must ensure that all crew members are properly trained and that they are performing their duties effectively. The ship captain is also responsible for managing the ship's budget, making sure that expenses are kept under control and that the ship is running efficiently.

To become a ship captain, a person must have a high school diploma or equivalent, complete a maritime training program, and gain experience working on ships. Depending on the type of vessel, the ship captain may need to obtain additional certifications or licenses, such as a Merchant Mariner's Credential or a Coast Guard license. They must also be physically fit to withstand the sometimes harsh conditions of life at sea.

One of the most interesting aspects of being a ship captain is the travel and adventure that comes with the job. Ship captains can travel to many different parts of the world, from major ports to remote locations. However, being a ship captain is not without its challenges. Life at sea can be physically and mentally demanding, and ship captains must be able to cope with long periods of isolation and the demands of the job.

SITE RELIABILITY ENGINEER

A Site Reliability Engineer (SRE) is a relatively new type of technical role that is quickly growing in importance in the field of technology. In a nutshell, an SRE's primary focus is to ensure that the systems and infrastructure that support a company's digital operations are running smoothly and efficiently.

An SRE is responsible for creating, developing, and maintaining the software tools and processes that allow applications and services to run seamlessly. The goal of an SRE is to increase the reliability of these systems by designing, implementing, and continuously improving the necessary tools, processes, and infrastructure.

To do this, SREs use a variety of skills, including computer programming, systems engineering, and data analysis. They work closely with other members of the technology team, such as software engineers, network administrators, and database administrators.

One of the key responsibilities of an SRE is to monitor the performance of the company's systems and infrastructure. They use a variety of tools and techniques to identify potential issues and troubleshoot problems as they arise. This includes analyzing log data, monitoring network traffic, and using machine learning algorithms to detect unusual patterns or behaviors.

In addition to monitoring and troubleshooting, SREs also work on designing and implementing new systems and infrastructure. This can include creating new software tools or automating manual processes, as well as developing new monitoring and analysis tools to help identify and diagnose issues more quickly.

Another key aspect of an SRE's role is to collaborate with other teams to ensure that changes and updates to the system are implemented smoothly. This includes working with software engineers to ensure that new code is deployed in a way that minimizes downtime and reduces the risk of errors.

Overall, the role of an SRE is to ensure that the digital operations of a company run smoothly, efficiently, and securely. They use a variety of tools and techniques to monitor and analyze systems and infrastructure, troubleshoot problems, and design and implement new systems and processes. As technology continues to play an increasingly important role in the world, the importance of SREs will only continue to grow.

Finally, an SRE is responsible for ensuring that the systems they manage are secure and protected against potential cyber-attacks. This includes implementing security measures such as firewalls, intrusion detection systems, and encryption protocols.

SOCIAL MEDIA MANAGER

Social media has become a crucial aspect of many people's daily lives, and businesses are no exception. With over 4.2 billion social media users around the world, it's no wonder that companies are utilizing social media platforms to connect with their customers and target audiences. This is where a social media manager comes in.

A social media manager is responsible for overseeing a company's social media presence, creating and curating content, developing social media strategies, and analyzing the performance of social media campaigns. They work to create a strong brand presence on social media and connect with customers in a meaningful way.

To be successful in their role, a social media manager must have a deep understanding of social media platforms, including Facebook, Twitter, Instagram, LinkedIn, and more. They also need to stay up-to-date on trends and changes to these platforms to ensure that their company's social media presence remains relevant and effective.

One of the primary responsibilities of a social media manager is to develop and execute social media campaigns. This involves creating content such as posts, images, and videos that will engage their target audience. Social media managers need to be skilled at crafting compelling messages that resonate with their audience and encourage them to engage with the brand. They also need to know when to post content, as different platforms have different peak usage times.

In addition to creating and curating content, social media managers must also engage with customers on social media. They need to respond to comments, messages, and reviews in a timely and professional manner, and ensure that the brand's voice is consistent across all interactions. This can be a challenging task, as social media can be a highly public and sometimes controversial platform.

Another important aspect of a social media manager's role is analyzing the performance of social media campaigns. They need to track metrics such as engagement rates, website traffic, and conversion rates to determine the effectiveness of their campaigns. Based on this data, they can adjust their strategies to ensure they are meeting their goals.

Finally, a social media manager needs to have excellent communication and interpersonal skills. They need to be able to work effectively with other departments, such as marketing and customer service, to ensure that the company's social media presence is consistent and aligned with overall business goals.

SOCIAL WORKER

Social workers are professionals who work with individuals, families, and communities to promote social change, improve the quality of life, and support people who are experiencing personal or societal difficulties. They work in various settings, such as hospitals, schools, government agencies, non-profit organizations, and private practices.

One of the primary roles of a social worker is to provide direct services to clients. They may work with individuals, families, or groups to help them cope with various challenges, such as poverty, homelessness, abuse, addiction, or mental illness. They may conduct assessments, develop treatment plans, provide counseling, and connect clients with community resources.

Social workers also play an important role in advocating for social change. They identify social problems and develop and implement policies and programs to address them. For example, they may work with community groups to improve access to healthcare or education, or advocate for policies that promote social justice and human rights.

Another important role of social workers is to help people navigate complex systems, such as healthcare, education, and the legal system. They may provide information and support to help people access services and resources, and help them understand and navigate the various processes and procedures involved.

Social workers also play an important role in research and evaluation. They may conduct research to identify social problems and develop interventions, and evaluate programs to determine their effectiveness. This research can help inform policy and practice, and improve the lives of people in the community.

There are many different types of social workers, each with their own areas of expertise. Some social workers specialize in working with children and families, while others work with the elderly, people with disabilities, or those who have experienced trauma. Some social workers work in the field of mental health, while others work in public health or in the criminal justice system.

In addition to the many different roles and specializations, social work is a profession that requires a strong commitment to social justice and a desire to make a positive impact on the lives of others. It can be a challenging but rewarding career, with the opportunity to help people in need and effect real change in the community.

SOFTWARE DEVELOPER

Software developers, also known as software engineers or programmers, take care of creating, designing, testing, and maintaining software programs that run on computers, mobile devices, and other electronic devices. These programs can be used for a wide range of purposes, from entertainment and gaming to finance and business. Software developers use programming languages like Java, Python, C++, and Ruby to write the code that makes these programs work.

One of the main roles of a software developer is to design and create software programs from scratch. This involves working with a team of other developers, as well as project managers, to identify the needs of the software and design a system that meets those needs. The software must be designed in a way that is efficient, easy to use, and reliable, so that users can operate it without any issues.

Once the design is complete, software developers write the code that makes the program work. This is often a complex process that requires a great deal of technical expertise. Developers use various programming languages to create the software code, and they must ensure that the code is accurate, efficient, and free of bugs or errors. To do this, they use debugging tools and other specialized software to test the program and fix any issues that may arise.

Software developers also work to maintain and improve existing software programs. This involves analyzing the code and identifying areas where the software could be made more efficient, as well as fixing any bugs or errors that may arise over time. As technology advances and new updates become available, developers must be prepared to adapt the software to keep up with these changes.

In addition to designing and creating software programs, developers also work closely with clients to understand their needs and identify any issues that may arise. They must be able to communicate technical concepts to non-technical individuals in a way that is clear and understandable. This can involve working with project managers, other developers, and clients to ensure that the software is designed and implemented to meet the needs of all stakeholders.

To be a successful software developer, one must have strong technical skills, a deep understanding of programming languages, and the ability to work collaboratively with others. They must also be able to think creatively and be able to solve complex problems, as well as work well under pressure and meet tight deadlines.

SOUND ENGINEER

A sound engineer is a professional who is responsible for the technical aspects of audio production. Their job is to ensure that sound recordings and live performances sound clear, balanced, and pleasing to the ear. They work on a variety of projects, ranging from music albums to TV and film productions to live events like concerts and theater performances.

One of the main tasks of a sound engineer is to set up and operate audio equipment, such as microphones, speakers, and recording devices. They work with various types of software and hardware to record, edit, and mix audio files. They use different techniques to manipulate sound, such as equalization, compression, and reverb, to achieve the desired sound quality.

Sound engineers also work with performers, directors, and other professionals to achieve the desired sound for a particular production. They collaborate with musicians, singers, actors, and other performers to capture and enhance their performances. For example, they might work with a singer to ensure that their vocals sound clear and powerful in a recorded track or live performance.

In live events, sound engineers play a critical role in ensuring that the sound is distributed evenly throughout the audience. They are responsible for setting up and testing the sound system, placing speakers in the right positions, and adjusting the volume and quality of sound. They need to be able to work under pressure, troubleshoot problems quickly, and make on-the-spot adjustments to ensure that everything runs smoothly.

Sound engineers also need to have excellent communication skills, as they often work with other professionals who may not have a technical background. They need to be able to explain technical concepts in a way that is easy to understand for their clients and colleagues.

In addition to technical skills, sound engineers also need to have a creative and artistic sensibility. They need to be able to listen carefully to different sounds and understand how to manipulate them to create the desired effect. They need to be able to work collaboratively with other professionals to achieve a cohesive artistic vision for a project.

In summary, a sound engineer is a technical professional who works in the field of audio production. They are responsible for setting up and operating audio equipment, recording and editing sound files, and ensuring that the sound quality is of high standard. They work on a variety of projects, from music albums to live events, and need to have a combination of technical, creative, and communication skills to succeed in the field.

SPEECH THERAPIST

A speech therapist, also known as a speech-language pathologist, is a healthcare professional who works with people of all ages to improve their communication abilities. Speech therapists help individuals overcome speech, language, and swallowing disorders, which can affect their daily life and their ability to interact with others. They work in a variety of settings, including schools, hospitals, private practices, and rehabilitation centers.

Speech therapists use a variety of techniques to evaluate and treat their patients. They begin by assessing the patient's speech and language skills, as well as their ability to understand and express language. They may ask the patient to repeat words or sentences, or they may use specialized tools and technology to evaluate the patient's speech, such as a computer-based language analysis system.

Once they have identified the patient's needs, speech therapists develop a personalized treatment plan to help them overcome their specific communication challenges. They work with their patients to help them improve their ability to communicate, whether it be by improving their pronunciation, grammar, or vocabulary. They also help patients develop the skills needed to understand and respond to language.

Speech therapists also work with patients who have swallowing disorders. These patients may have difficulty swallowing food or drink, or they may have trouble chewing or moving their tongue and mouth. Speech therapists use a variety of techniques to help patients overcome these challenges, including exercises that help improve their swallowing abilities.

In addition to their work with patients, speech therapists also work with family members and caregivers to help them understand the patient's needs and how they can support them. They may provide education and training to family members on how to best communicate with their loved one, or they may provide advice on how to make modifications to the home environment to better support the patient's communication needs.

Speech therapy can make a significant impact on a person's life. By improving communication abilities, speech therapists can help their patients to develop stronger relationships, improve their self-esteem, and even increase their job prospects. They work with individuals of all ages, from young children who are just learning to speak to older adults who may have experienced a stroke or other medical condition that affects their ability to communicate.

SPORTS ANNOUNCER

A sports announcer is a broadcasting professional who reports and provides commentary on sporting events. They play an essential role in bringing the excitement of sports to millions of viewers around the world. Whether they work for a local radio station or a major television network, sports announcers have an important job to do, and they take it very seriously.

To become a sports announcer, one must have a deep knowledge of the sports they cover, a clear speaking voice, and a knack for storytelling. They must also be able to work well under pressure and be able to improvise when things don't go as planned. Sports announcers must be able to convey their excitement and passion for the game to their viewers and listeners.

One of the primary responsibilities of a sports announcer is to provide a play-by-play account of the action on the field or court. This means describing the movement of the ball or puck, the positioning of the players, and any key plays that occur during the game. They must also keep track of the score and the time remaining in the game.

In addition to providing a play-by-play account, sports announcers also provide color commentary. This involves giving their opinions and insights on the game, the players, and the strategies being employed by both teams. They also provide context and historical information that helps viewers understand the significance of the game and the events taking place on the field.

To prepare for a game, sports announcers spend a considerable amount of time researching the teams, the players, and the history of the sport. They review game statistics, study player biographies, and research the latest trends in the sport. This helps them provide insightful commentary during the game and helps to enhance the viewer's understanding of the sport.

During a game, sports announcers work closely with producers, directors, and other members of the production team to ensure that the broadcast runs smoothly. They must also be able to work well with their co-announcers, providing a seamless flow of commentary throughout the game.

Sports announcers are also often involved in the marketing and promotion of their broadcasts. They participate in promotional events, give interviews to the media, and work with sponsors to promote their broadcasts. They must also be able to work with social media and other digital platforms to engage with fans and build their brand.

STAND-UP COMEDIAN

Stand-up comedy is an art form that has been around for many decades, and it's no secret that comedians are some of the most talented and creative people in the world. However, there is a lot more to being a stand-up comedian than just telling jokes on stage.

At its core, stand-up comedy is all about making people laugh. This means that a stand-up comedian spends a lot of time writing, practicing, and performing material that they hope will be funny and relatable to their audience. The material can be anything from personal anecdotes and observational humor to social commentary and satire.

The first step for a stand-up comedian is to write their material. This can be a time-consuming process that involves a lot of trial and error. Comedians may start with a general idea or concept and then work to build out the material through brainstorming, writing, and editing. They'll also need to consider the delivery of the jokes, such as timing, pacing, and tone.

Once they've written their material, the comedian will need to practice it in front of an audience. This is where open mic nights come into play. Open mic nights are events where comedians can try out their material in front of a live audience. This is a great way for comedians to gauge how well their material is working and make changes as needed.

Of course, not every joke is going to land with every audience. When a joke doesn't work, it's up to the comedian to keep the show moving and not let it affect their performance. This is where the art of improvisation comes in. Comedians need to be able to think on their feet and come up with new material or a witty comment to keep the audience engaged. Stand-up comedy is not just about the content, but also about the delivery, stage presence, and persona of the comedian. Some comedians have a more casual, conversational style, while others are more high-energy and animated.

In addition to writing and performing, stand-up comedians also need to be skilled at marketing themselves. This means developing a brand, creating a website and social media presence, and networking with other comedians and industry professionals. Comedians also need to be able to manage their own careers and negotiate deals with bookers, agents, and other stakeholders.

While being a stand-up comedian can be a rewarding and fulfilling career, it's not for everyone. The lifestyle can be unpredictable, with late nights and travel being common. It's also a very competitive field, with many comedians vying for the same opportunities and gigs.

STATICIAN

A statistician is a professional who uses mathematical and statistical techniques to analyze and interpret data. The work of statisticians can be found in an endless number of fields, including finance, healthcare, sports, and politics, among others. Statisticians can work in academic or research settings, for private companies, government agencies, or non-profit organizations.

One of the key roles of a statistician is to collect, analyze, and interpret data. This involves designing surveys, experiments, and other research studies to gather the data necessary to answer specific questions or solve problems. Statisticians also use software and programming languages to organize, clean, and manipulate data, making sure it is accurate and complete before conducting any analyses.

Statisticians also play an important role in communicating their findings to others, including fellow statisticians, scientists, business leaders, policymakers, and the general public. They might create reports, presentations, and visualizations that summarize the results of their analyses, making the data accessible and meaningful to those who need it. In this way, statisticians help decision-makers make informed choices and improve outcomes in a wide variety of fields.

One example of how statisticians work is in public health. Statisticians might help design and analyze studies to determine the prevalence of a particular disease or identify risk factors for certain conditions. They might also work with public health officials to monitor disease outbreaks or evaluate the effectiveness of interventions such as vaccines or public health campaigns.

In finance, statisticians play a critical role in assessing risk and making informed investment decisions. They might develop models to forecast future trends in financial markets, evaluate the performance of investment portfolios, or analyze consumer behavior to identify new business opportunities. By using statistical models to identify patterns and make predictions, statisticians help investors and businesses make informed decisions that maximize their returns and minimize their risks.

Statisticians also play an important role in sports, helping coaches and managers make strategic decisions based on data. For example, a baseball team might use statistical analyses to identify the most effective batting order, evaluate player performance, or identify new talent. By analyzing large amounts of data on player performance, statisticians can help sports teams gain a competitive edge and improve their chances of success.

STUNT ACTOR

Stunt actors are the daredevils of the film and television industry, performing physically demanding and potentially dangerous stunts that add excitement and realism to action scenes. They work closely with the director, choreographers, and actors to ensure that the stunts are executed safely and accurately.

A stunt actor's job is to perform stunts in place of the main actor, whose safety is a top priority. This means that they need to have a high level of physical fitness, as well as expertise in a range of specialized skills, such as martial arts, gymnastics, horseback riding, and driving.

Stunt actors typically start by learning basic stunt techniques and working their way up to more advanced maneuvers. They may spend years perfecting their craft and building their portfolio, performing in smaller productions and earning a reputation little by little.

In addition to their physical abilities, stunt actors also need to have strong communication and collaboration skills. They work closely with the director and choreographers to understand the vision for the scene and to ensure that the stunt fits seamlessly into the larger narrative of the production.

Stunt actors also need to be adept at working with a range of equipment and technology, from harnesses and wires to special effects and pyrotechnics. They need to be able to perform complex stunts while wearing bulky or restrictive safety gear, and they need to be able to work quickly and efficiently to ensure that the production stays on schedule.

Perhaps one of the most exciting aspects of being a stunt actor is the opportunity to work on a wide range of productions, from high-budget action movies to television shows, commercials, and even live events. Every production presents new challenges and opportunities, and stunt actors need to be adaptable and versatile in order to succeed in this fast-paced and unpredictable industry.

Stunt actors also need to be able to maintain a high level of physical fitness and endurance, as they may be required to perform demanding stunts in a range of weather conditions and environments. This means that they need to be dedicated to their craft and committed to maintaining a healthy and active lifestyle.

Overall, the life of a stunt actor is both physically demanding and thrilling. It requires a unique combination of skills, expertise, and personality, as well as a willingness to take risks and push oneself to the limit. But for those who are passionate about the craft, it can be an incredibly rewarding and exciting career.

SURGEON

Surgeons are highly skilled medical professionals who specialize in the diagnosis, treatment, and management of surgical conditions. They are responsible for performing surgical procedures to treat diseases, injuries, and deformities, and to improve the overall health of their patients.

Surgeons typically work in hospitals, medical centers, and clinics, and may focus on a particular area of expertise, such as cardiovascular surgery, neurosurgery, orthopedic surgery, or plastic surgery. They work closely with other medical professionals, including anesthesiologists, and nurses to ensure that their patients receive the best possible care.

One of the key responsibilities of a surgeon is to assess the patient's condition and determine the most appropriate course of treatment. This may involve reviewing the patient's medical history, conducting diagnostic tests, and consulting with other medical professionals. Once the diagnosis has been made, the surgeon will develop a treatment plan that may involve surgery, medication, or other forms of therapy.

If surgery is deemed necessary, the surgeon will perform the procedure using a variety of tools and techniques. They may use minimally invasive techniques, such as laparoscopic or robotic surgery, which involve making small incisions and using a camera to guide the surgical instruments. Or they may use more traditional open surgery techniques, which involve making a larger incision to access the affected area.

During the surgery, the surgeon will carefully monitor the patient's vital signs and ensure that they remain stable. They will also work closely with the other members of the surgical team to ensure that the procedure is performed safely and effectively.

After the surgery, the surgeon will monitor the patient's recovery and work to manage any complications that may arise. They may also prescribe medications or other forms of therapy to help manage pain and aid in the healing process.

In addition to performing surgeries, surgeons also work to educate patients about their conditions and treatment options. They may also conduct research to develop new surgical techniques or to improve existing ones, in order to better treat their patients and advance the field of surgery as a whole.

Becoming a surgeon requires extensive education and training. In addition to earning a medical degree, surgeons must complete a residency program in their chosen area of expertise. This involves additional years of training, during which time they will work closely with experienced surgeons to gain hands-on experience in the operating room.

TAILOR

A tailor is a professional who specializes in designing, fitting, and altering garments. The term "tailor" comes from the French word "tailleur," which means cutter, and the occupation of tailoring has a rich history dating back to ancient times. Today, tailors work in places from small boutique shops to high-end fashion houses, and their skills are in high demand for people who want clothing that fits well and looks great.

One of the primary responsibilities of a tailor is to measure and fit clients for clothing. This process involves taking precise measurements of a client's body, including their chest, waist, hips, and inseam. The tailor then uses these measurements to create a pattern for the garment and cut the fabric accordingly. In addition to fitting new clothing, tailors also offer alteration services, which involves modifying existing garments to fit better.

Tailors work with a variety of different materials, including wool, silk, cotton, and synthetic fabrics. They use specialized tools such as scissors, measuring tape, and sewing machines to create high-quality clothing. They may also be skilled in hand-sewing techniques such as embroidery and beading. Some tailors specialize in creating custom suits, dresses, or other formal wear, while others focus on more casual clothing.

In addition to technical skills, tailors must have excellent communication skills to work with clients effectively. They must be able to listen carefully to clients' requests and offer advice on style, fit, and fabric choices. They must also be able to explain complex alterations and modifications in a way that is easily understood by clients.

One of the most interesting aspects of being a tailor is the creativity involved in the job. Tailors have the opportunity to work with clients to create unique and personalized garments that reflect the client's individual style and personality. This requires a high level of creativity and attention to detail, as well as the ability to work with a variety of different fabrics and designs.

Tailors may also have the opportunity to work on high-profile projects, such as creating costumes for movies, theater productions, or fashion shows. These projects can be challenging, as they often require working within tight deadlines and creating garments that are both functional and visually striking.

Another interesting aspect of being a tailor is the opportunity to work with a wide range of clients. Tailors may work with people from all walks of life, from executives and politicians to artists and performers. This can be both challenging and rewarding, as tailors must be able to adapt their skills and approach to fit the unique needs of each client.

TAXIDERMIST

Taxidermy is the art of preserving animals or birds' skins, feathers, and other parts of their bodies by stuffing and mounting them. It is a unique craft that requires a keen eye for detail and a delicate touch.

Taxidermists are professionals who create lifelike representations of animals that have passed away, either through hunting or natural causes. Taxidermists use a variety of techniques to preserve and mount the animal, including skinning, tanning, sculpting, painting, and sewing.

To begin, the taxidermist carefully removes the skin from the animal's body, making sure to keep it as intact as possible. Once the skin is removed, the taxidermist treats it with a solution to prevent decay and preserve the fur, feathers, or scales. The skin is then stretched over a form, which is shaped to match the animal's original size and shape.

The taxidermist also has to take care to position the animal's limbs, head, and other features to create a natural and lifelike pose. This can involve using wires or other supports to ensure the animal is correctly positioned.

Once the skin is mounted, the taxidermist will paint the eyes and other features to create a realistic appearance. The result is a unique work of art that can be displayed in homes, museums, or other places.

Beyond creating art, taxidermy also has practical applications. For example, it is often used in scientific research to study animal behavior, anatomy, and ecology. It also plays a role in conservation efforts, as taxidermists may mount specimens of endangered animals for educational purposes.

In addition to preserving animal skins, taxidermists may also create other objects, such as fish mounts, skulls, and antlers. They may also collaborate with collectors to create custom pieces, such as a recreation of a beloved pet.

Becoming a taxidermist requires a unique set of skills and knowledge. Taxidermists must have an understanding of animal anatomy, an eye for detail, and the ability to work with a variety of materials. They must also be patient and precise, as the work requires a great deal of concentration and attention to detail.

In terms of education and training, many taxidermists learn the craft through apprenticeships or by attending specialized schools or workshops. Some taxidermists also pursue degrees in biology or related fields to deepen their understanding of animal anatomy and behavior.

TEACHER

Teachers play an important role in society by shaping the minds of future generations. At its core, a teacher's job is to educate and inspire students, but the specifics of what a teacher does can vary greatly depending on their subject, age group, and setting.

Elementary school teachers, for example, typically teach multiple subjects to a single class of students, while high school teachers may specialize in one or two subjects and teach multiple classes. Additionally, some teachers work in public schools, while others may work in private schools, charter schools, or even in online or home-schooling settings.

Regardless of the specifics, the job of a teacher is both challenging and rewarding. In order to be an effective teacher, one must have strong subject matter knowledge, excellent communication and interpersonal skills, and a passion for helping students learn.

One of the primary responsibilities of a teacher is to plan and deliver engaging lessons to their students. This may involve creating lesson plans, developing activities and assignments, and adapting their teaching style to meet the needs of different types of learners. A good teacher is able to effectively communicate complex concepts in a way that is understandable and relatable to students of all ages.

In addition to lesson planning and delivery, teachers also have a responsibility to assess their students' understanding and progress. This may involve grading assignments and tests, providing feedback to students, and offering additional support to those who are struggling. Effective teachers are able to identify the individual needs of their students and provide support and guidance to help them succeed.

Another important aspect of a teacher's job is to provide a safe and supportive learning environment for their students. This may involve managing classroom behavior, mediating conflicts, and fostering a positive and inclusive atmosphere. Teachers may also be responsible for providing emotional support to their students, particularly in cases where a student is dealing with personal or family issues that may be affecting their academic performance.

In addition to these day-to-day responsibilities, teachers also play an important role in the larger education community. This may involve attending professional development workshops or conferences, collaborating with other teachers to share best practices and resources, or advocating for education policy changes that benefit students.

TECHNICAL WRITER

Technical writers are professionals who specialize in creating documentation for technical or scientific materials. These documents can range from user manuals to technical reports to grant proposals. Technical writers work in various fields, including technology, engineering, medicine, and science.

The primary function of a technical writer is to communicate complex information to a non-technical audience. This requires them to have a deep understanding of the subject matter they are writing about and the ability to explain it in a clear and concise way.

In addition to technical knowledge, technical writers must also be skilled in writing and communication. They must be able to organize information in a logical and easy-to-understand way, as well as write in a clear and concise manner. Technical writers must also be proficient in the use of technical writing tools, such as graphics, charts, and diagrams, to help explain complex concepts.

One of the primary tasks of a technical writer is to create user manuals or documentation for software, hardware, or other products. This can include everything from step-by-step instructions for installing and using software, to safety instructions for industrial machinery. These manuals must be easy to read and understand, even for people who are not familiar with the product or technical jargon.

Technical writers may also be involved in writing proposals for research grants or other funding opportunities. In these cases, they must be able to communicate complex technical information in a way that is accessible to non-technical reviewers. They may work with research scientists or engineers to write grant proposals that effectively communicate the potential impact of the research.

Another area where technical writers are often employed is in the creation of technical reports. These reports can be used for a variety of purposes, such as communicating the results of scientific research or summarizing the findings of an engineering project. Technical writers work with subject matter experts to gather and analyze data, and then create a report that summarizes the findings in an easy-to-understand format.

Technical writers are also responsible for creating marketing materials, such as brochures, white papers, and case studies. These materials are designed to explain the benefits and features of a product or service, and to convince potential customers that it is the right choice for them. Technical writers must be able to write persuasive copy that is both informative and engaging.

TELECOMMUNICATIONS ENGINEER

Telecommunications engineering is a field that involves designing and supporting communication systems, such as telephones, cell phones, and the internet. Telecommunications engineers use a combination of technical and creative skills to create new ways for people to connect with each other and access information.

At its core, telecommunications engineering is about designing and building systems that transmit and receive data. This includes voice, video, and text communication, as well as large-scale data transfer for applications like the internet of things and cloud computing. These systems use a wide range of technologies, including wired and wireless networks, satellite communications, and fiber optics.

The work of a telecommunications engineer can vary depending on their area of focus. For example, a wireless engineer might work on improving cellular network coverage or developing new wireless technologies, while a fiber optic engineer might be responsible for designing high-speed internet connections for businesses or residential areas. A telecommunications engineer might also work on developing software to control and monitor communication systems, or they might oversee the construction and installation of physical components like antennas and cabling.

One of the main challenges facing telecommunications engineers is keeping up with the constantly-evolving landscape of technology. The industry moves quickly, with new technologies and standards emerging all the time. Engineers need to stay up-to-date with the latest developments in order to keep their skills relevant and maintain the ability to design and build cutting-edge systems.

Another key challenge for telecommunications engineers is the need to balance competing priorities, such as reliability, speed, and cost. For example, a wireless network might need to be designed to provide the best possible signal strength and speed while also minimizing interference from other devices and keeping costs under control.

To succeed in this field, a telecommunications engineer needs to have a strong foundation in math and science, as well as strong problem-solving and analytical skills. They should also be creative and able to think outside the box, as developing innovative new communication technologies often requires a fresh perspective.

Overall, telecommunications engineering is an exciting and constantly-evolving field that plays a crucial role in shaping the way we communicate and access information. With the rapid pace of innovation in this area, there are plenty of opportunities for skilled professionals to make a real impact in the world of technology and beyond.

TRADER

Trading can be a fascinating and dynamic profession that involves buying and selling various financial instruments in order to make a profit. Traders are experts in the markets, using their knowledge of economic trends, financial analysis, and risk management to make informed decisions about when and how to invest. There are many different types of traders, including stock traders, foreign exchange (forex) traders, and commodity traders.

At its core, trading involves buying low and selling high. Traders carefully study financial markets to identify trends and opportunities, seeking to buy assets at a low price and sell them at a higher price when the value increases. This can be done over the course of a few seconds, hours, or days or weeks, depending on the type of trading being done.

There are many different factors that can influence the price of financial instruments, including economic indicators, company earnings reports, political events, and global crises. Successful traders are able to stay up-to-date on these factors and anticipate how they may affect the markets, allowing them to make informed decisions and potentially profit from market movements.

Traders often work for financial institutions such as banks, hedge funds, and investment firms, but some may work independently as well. While many traders work in offices, some may work from home or remotely. The hours can be long and the work can be stressful, but for those with a passion for financial markets, it can be rewarding.

Traders use a variety of tools and techniques to make their trades. These can include technical analysis, which involves studying charts and graphs to identify trends, and fundamental analysis, which involves studying economic data, company reports, and other financial information to assess the value of an asset. Traders may also use a variety of trading strategies, such as trend following, swing trading, and day trading.

In addition to making trades, traders must also manage risk. Trading can be a high-risk profession, and traders must be able to manage the risk of potential losses. This can involve setting stop-loss orders, which automatically sell an asset if it drops below a certain price, as well as using other risk management techniques to limit exposure to potential losses.

Traders must also stay up-to-date on changes in financial regulations, as well as technological advancements that may impact the markets. The rise of online trading platforms, for example, has made it easier for individual investors to participate in the markets, which has in turn increased competition for professional traders.

TRAVEL AGENT

A travel agent is a professional who helps clients plan, book, and manage their travel arrangements. They are knowledgeable about various destinations, travel options, and the travel industry in general. While many people think that the internet has made travel agents obsolete, there are still many benefits to using a travel agent, especially for more complex travel itineraries.

One of the primary tasks of a travel agent is to help clients plan their trip. They work with clients to understand their travel needs and preferences and then provide recommendations on destinations, travel options, and activities. They are also responsible for booking flights, hotels, rental cars, and other travel arrangements. They ensure that all of the details are taken care of and that everything runs smoothly.

One of the most significant benefits of using a travel agent is that they can save clients time and money. Travel agents have access to a wealth of information and resources, including exclusive deals and discounts that may not be available to the public. They can also help clients avoid costly mistakes, such as booking flights with inconvenient layovers or hotels in less desirable areas. They can often find more affordable travel options that clients may not have been aware of on their own.

Another benefit of working with a travel agent is that they can provide a more personalized experience. They take the time to get to know their clients and their travel preferences, so they can tailor their recommendations accordingly. They may even be able to arrange unique experiences that would be difficult for clients to book on their own, such as private tours or behind-the-scenes access to popular attractions.

In addition to helping clients plan and book their trips, travel agents also provide support and assistance throughout the entire travel process. They may offer advice on packing, provide information on local customs and culture, and help clients navigate any unexpected issues that may arise during their trip.

To be a successful travel agent, one must be knowledgeable about various destinations, travel options, and the travel industry as a whole. They should have excellent communication and interpersonal skills, be highly organized and detail-oriented, and be able to work well under pressure. Many travel agents have a passion for travel themselves and enjoy sharing their experiences and expertise with their clients.

TRUCK DRIVER

Truck drivers are an essential part of the transportation industry, responsible for safely and efficiently moving goods across the country. They play a crucial role in delivering the products that keep our economy and our lives running smoothly.

Truck drivers, also known as heavy and tractor-trailer truck drivers, operate large commercial vehicles to transport goods over long distances. They may work for trucking companies, manufacturers, wholesalers, or retailers. Some truck drivers work for themselves and run their own businesses.

Before setting off on a trip, truck drivers need to inspect their trucks and cargo to make sure everything is in working order and secure. They must also plan their route, taking into account the type of cargo they are carrying, weather conditions, and traffic patterns. During their trips, they must abide by federal and state regulations that dictate how long they can drive and how much rest they need to take.

One of the main challenges that truck drivers face is the long hours they spend on the road. Many truckers work long hours and spend weeks away from home. This can be a difficult lifestyle, and drivers must have the discipline and endurance to stay alert and focused while on the road.

Truck drivers need a variety of skills to do their jobs effectively. They must have excellent driving skills and be able to maneuver their vehicles in all types of weather and road conditions. They must also be skilled at managing their time and staying on schedule, as their deliveries must arrive on time to ensure that supply chains continue to function smoothly.

To become a truck driver, individuals must obtain a commercial driver's license (CDL). This involves passing a written exam and a driving test. Some employers may also require a high school diploma or equivalent.

Truck drivers can expect to earn a decent living. Pay can vary depending on the type of cargo being transported, the distance traveled, and the level of experience of the driver.

In summary, truck drivers are an integral part of the transportation industry, responsible for the safe and timely delivery of goods across the country. They need to have excellent driving skills, strong time management abilities, and effective communication and customer service skills. While the long hours and time away from home can be challenging, truck drivers play a vital role in keeping the economy running smoothly.

TV PRODUCER

A TV producer manages the creation, development, and production of television shows. From reality TV shows to documentaries and dramas, a TV producer works behind the scenes to bring the best content to viewers. The job of a TV producer is diverse and requires a wide range of skills, from creative to technical.

The role of a TV producer begins with the idea. They work with writers, directors, and other creative professionals to develop concepts for TV shows. The producer is responsible for creating a compelling story or idea that can be translated into a visual medium. They work with writers to create scripts, and they oversee the casting process to ensure the right talent is selected for the roles.

Once the show is in pre-production, the TV producer oversees the creative direction, ensuring that the vision of the show is being realized. They work with the director to make sure that the look and feel of the show is consistent with the concept. They also work with the set designers, costume designers, and other professionals to create the right aesthetic for the show.

During production, the TV producer is responsible for keeping the show on schedule and within budget. They work with the crew to ensure that everything is running smoothly, and they make decisions on the spot to ensure that the show stays on track. They also work with the talent to make sure that they are delivering their lines and performing at their best.

After filming is complete, the TV producer works on post-production. This involves editing, sound design, and special effects. The producer works with the editing team to ensure that the show is cut together in a way that tells the story effectively. They also work with the sound design team to ensure that the audio is crisp and clear.

In addition to creative responsibilities, TV producers must also be business-savvy. They work closely with networks and studios to secure funding for their projects, negotiate contracts, and sell their ideas. They must also be able to manage budgets effectively to ensure that their shows are profitable.

TV producers must be creative, organized, and have excellent communication skills. They must be able to manage large teams of people, and they must be able to make quick decisions on the spot. They also need to have a good understanding of the technical aspects of TV production, such as cameras, lighting, and sound design.

USER EXPERIENCE (UX) DESIGNER

A UX (user experience) designer is responsible for creating digital products, such as websites, applications, and software, that are easy and intuitive for users to navigate and use. The goal of a UX designer is to make the user's experience as smooth and enjoyable as possible. They need to have a good understanding of both the technology behind the product as well as the needs and behaviors of the users who will be interacting with it.

One of the main responsibilities of a UX designer is to conduct research to understand the users and their needs. This may involve interviewing users, conducting surveys, and analyzing data to gain insights into what users want and need from the product. This research is used to guide the design of the product and ensure that it meets the needs of the target audience.

Once the research has been conducted, the UX designer will create wireframes and prototypes to show the layout and functionality of the product. These designs are often created using specialized software such as Sketch, Adobe XD, or Figma. The designer will often collaborate with other team members such as developers and graphic designers to ensure that the product meets the design specifications.

The UX designer must also consider the overall branding of the product, making sure that the design aligns with the company's visual identity and brand standards. They may also work closely with marketing and content teams to ensure that the product is marketed effectively to the target audience.

During the development phase of the product, the UX designer will test and evaluate the product to ensure that it is meeting the needs of the users. They may conduct usability tests, A/B testing, and user acceptance testing to gather feedback and make improvements. This testing phase is critical for identifying any issues and making sure that the product is as user-friendly as possible.

Another important aspect of a UX designer's role is to stay up-to-date with the latest design trends and technologies. They need to be aware of new developments in design software, emerging technologies, and changes in user behavior. This helps them to stay ahead of the curve and ensure that their products are always meeting the needs of users.

One key skill that a UX designer needs is excellent communication. They must be able to communicate their design ideas and decisions to stakeholders and team members, often using visual aids such as wireframes, prototypes, and presentations. They must also be able to take feedback from others and use it to improve the product.

VETERINARIAN

Veterinarians are medical professionals who specialize in caring for animals. They provide a wide range of services, including routine checkups, preventative care, diagnosis and treatment of illnesses and injuries, and surgery. Vets work with animals of all shapes and sizes, including household pets, farm animals, zoo animals, and even some exotic species.

One of the primary roles of a veterinarian is to ensure that animals stay healthy. This involves performing routine checkups and screenings to monitor the overall health of an animal, and to detect any early signs of illness or disease. Vets will also recommend preventative measures, such as vaccinations and parasite control, to keep animals in good health.

In addition to preventative care, veterinarians are also responsible for diagnosing and treating illnesses and injuries in animals. This can include everything from minor issues such as cuts and scrapes, to more serious conditions like cancer or chronic illnesses. Veterinarians will conduct physical exams, run diagnostic tests, and develop treatment plans to help animals recover from their ailments.

Another important aspect of a veterinarian's work is surgical procedures. Vets may perform surgeries to remove tumors, repair broken bones, or to spay or neuter animals. They may also perform emergency surgeries in situations where an animal's life is in danger, such as in cases of severe trauma or internal bleeding.

Aside from the physical care of animals, veterinarians are also responsible for educating pet owners on proper animal care. This includes providing advice on nutrition, exercise, and other preventative care measures, as well as answering questions and concerns regarding their pets' health.

Veterinarians must also be skilled communicators, as they often have to work closely with pet owners and other veterinary professionals. They must be able to explain complex medical conditions and procedures in layman's terms, and provide compassionate support to pet owners during difficult times, such as when a pet is seriously ill or injured.

The work of a veterinarian is not limited to the traditional veterinary office or clinic. Many vets work in other settings, such as on farms or ranches, or in zoos and aquariums. In these situations, veterinarians may be responsible for a broader range of animals, and may need to be available around the clock to provide emergency care.

VIDEO PRODUCER

A video producer is a professional who oversees the production of videos, from conception to completion. They are responsible for all aspects of the production process, including brainstorming ideas, creating a script, coordinating filming, managing the budget, and ensuring the finished product is of the highest quality.

One of the most important roles of a video producer is to work with the client or the creative team to identify the goals of the project. This might involve understanding the message that the client wants to convey, the target audience, and the budget. Once these goals have been established, the producer will start to create a plan for how the project will be executed.

The video producer must be able to manage multiple tasks and work collaboratively with a team. They must be skilled in project management, budgeting, and scheduling, as they will be responsible for ensuring that the project stays on track and on budget.

In pre-production, the video producer works with the creative team to develop the concept, write the script, create storyboards, and hire the necessary cast and crew. They must also secure the necessary permits and location releases.

During production, the video producer supervises the filming, ensures that everything runs smoothly, and solves any problems that arise. They work with the director to ensure that the script is followed and that the vision of the project is achieved.

Post-production involves editing the footage and creating the final product. The video producer works closely with the post-production team to ensure that the final product is of the highest quality. They must review the rough cuts, make revisions, and approve the final edit.

Aside from the creative aspects of video production, a video producer must also have excellent communication and interpersonal skills, as they will be working with a variety of people, from clients to actors to crew members. They must be able to manage multiple tasks and work collaboratively with a team.

Video producers can work on a variety of projects, from commercials and music videos to feature films and documentaries. They may work in-house for a production company, for an advertising agency, or as a freelancer.

In today's digital age, video is a powerful tool for communicating a message or telling a story. The role of the video producer is critical in bringing these ideas to life, and the demand for talented producers is only growing.

VIRTUAL REALITY DEVELOPER

Virtual reality (VR) has exploded in popularity over the last few years, with applications ranging from gaming and entertainment to education and training. Behind every great VR experience is a skilled virtual reality developer, a professional responsible for creating the 3D environments and interactive elements that make VR come to life.

At a high level, a virtual reality developer is responsible for designing and creating the software that powers VR experiences. This involves creating 3D models, animations, and user interfaces, as well as programming the interactions between the user and the virtual environment. They work with a range of tools and technologies, including game engines, 3D modeling software, and programming languages like C++ and JavaScript.

One of the key skills required for virtual reality development is a strong understanding of 3D modeling and animation. This involves creating 3D models of objects, characters, and environments, and then animating them to bring them to life. Virtual reality developers also need to be skilled in the use of game engines, which are software frameworks designed to simplify the creation of interactive experiences. Common game engines used in VR development include Unity and Unreal Engine.

Another important aspect of virtual reality development is user interface design. Because users interact with VR environments in unique ways (often with hand-held controllers or even their own bodies), designing intuitive and user-friendly interfaces is crucial. VR developers need to have a deep understanding of user experience (UX) design principles and the ability to create intuitive interfaces that feel natural to use.

Programming is also a core aspect of virtual reality development. Developers need to have a strong grasp of programming languages like C++ and JavaScript, as well as the ability to use game engines to create interactive experiences. They also need to be skilled in debugging and troubleshooting, as even small errors in the code can cause significant issues in a VR experience.

Collaboration is key in VR development, as they usually work with artists, designers, and other developers. They need to have excellent communication skills, the ability to work well with others, and the ability to take and give constructive feedback.

In addition to technical skills, successful virtual reality developers need to be creative and innovative thinkers. VR is still a relatively new technology, and there is a lot of room for exploration and experimentation in this field. Developers who can think outside the box and come up with new and innovative ways to use VR technology are likely to be in high demand.

WAITER / WAITRESS

As anyone who has ever worked in a restaurant will tell you, waiting tables is no easy job. However, it can also be an incredibly rewarding and enjoyable career for those who are passionate about food, hospitality, and customer service. Waiters and waitresses are the frontline staff of any restaurant, responsible for greeting customers, taking orders, serving food and drinks, and ensuring that diners have an enjoyable experience.

The first thing a waiter or waitress will do when they arrive for their shift is to set up their station. This typically involves checking that they have enough clean plates, glasses, and silverware, and ensuring that everything is clean and presentable. They may also be responsible for setting up the dining room, arranging tables and chairs, and ensuring that the ambiance is just right.

Once the restaurant is open and customers begin to arrive, the waiter's or waitress's primary responsibility is to greet them and make them feel welcome. They will escort diners to their table, take their orders, and answer any questions they may have about the menu. A good waiter or waitress will be knowledgeable about the restaurant's dishes and ingredients and be able to make recommendations based on the customer's preferences.

Once the food is ready, the waiter or waitress will serve it to the customers, ensuring that each dish is presented beautifully and with attention to detail. They will also be responsible for serving drinks, refilling glasses, and checking on customers to ensure that they are satisfied with their meals.

Throughout the meal, the waiter or waitress will be responsible for keeping the dining area clean and tidy. They will clear empty plates and glasses, wipe down the table, and ensure that everything is in order for the next customers. At the end of the meal, the waiter or waitress will present the check to the customers and collect payment.

In addition to these core responsibilities, a good waiter or waitress will also be skilled in customer service, able to handle customer complaints or requests in a professional and courteous manner. They will also be organized and efficient, able to manage multiple tables at once and keep track of orders, payments, and other important details.

Many waiters and waitresses work in full-service restaurants, but the job can also be found in other hospitality and food service settings such as hotels, cafes, and bars. The work can be physically demanding, with long hours spent on your feet, but it can also be incredibly rewarding, especially for those who are passionate about food and hospitality.

WEB DEVELOPER

A web developer is a highly skilled professional who creates and maintains websites. They are responsible for designing, building, and maintaining websites, as well as ensuring that they are optimized for the best user experience. A web developer's role is to bring a website to life by taking an idea and turning it into a functional, user-friendly website.

A web developer's work often begins with understanding what the client or organization needs from the website. They then determine the technical requirements necessary to meet those needs. This can involve writing code in various programming languages, such as HTML, CSS, and JavaScript. They also work with web development tools and frameworks like Bootstrap, React, and Angular.

One of the most important roles of a web developer is to ensure that a website is user-friendly and easy to navigate. This means that they need to understand the psychology of how users interact with websites. They also need to have a keen eye for detail and design to create an aesthetically pleasing website that will engage visitors.

Web developers work on both the front-end and back-end of websites. The front-end refers to the user interface of a website, such as what a visitor sees when they access the website. The back-end is the behind-the-scenes functionality that makes the website work, such as the database, server, and other technical elements.

A web developer must ensure that the website is fully responsive, meaning that it is optimized for use on various devices, including desktops, laptops, tablets, and smartphones. They also need to ensure that the website is optimized for search engines, which involves making the website easily accessible and navigable for search engine crawlers.

Web developers often work collaboratively with designers, marketers, and other professionals to ensure that the website meets the client's needs and is aligned with their brand. They must also stay up-to-date with the latest trends in web development and technologies to stay competitive in the field.

Overall, web development is a challenging and dynamic field that requires creativity, technical expertise, and problem-solving skills. Web developers play a vital role in the digital landscape by creating websites that are functional, visually appealing, and optimized for the best user experience.

WELDER

Welding is the process of joining two or more pieces of metal or thermoplastics together using heat, pressure, or a combination of both. It is a critical aspect of many manufacturing, construction, and repair processes, and is used in a wide range of industries, including automotive, aerospace, construction, shipbuilding, and manufacturing.

Welding is a skilled trade that requires a high level of precision and attention to detail, as well as a thorough understanding of metallurgy, electricity, and heat transfer. Welders use a variety of tools and techniques to create strong, reliable bonds between metal components, and they must be able to work with a range of different materials and thicknesses.

The work of a welder can vary widely depending on the industry they work in, but generally involves the following tasks:

1. Reading blueprints and technical drawings to determine the type and amount of welding required, as well as the materials and tools needed to complete the job.

2. Selecting the appropriate welding technique for the job, such as MIG (metal inert gas), TIG (tungsten inert gas), or stick welding, based on the materials and thickness of the components being welded.

3. Positioning and securing the metal components to be welded using clamps, jigs, or other holding devices to ensure that they remain in place during the welding process.

4. Operating the welding equipment and monitoring the welding process to ensure that the weld is strong, even, and consistent, and that it conforms to the specifications of the job.

Welding is a physically demanding job that requires a great deal of skill and expertise. Welders must have good hand-eye coordination, as well as excellent manual dexterity and fine motor skills, in order to work with precision and accuracy. They must also be able to work in a variety of different environments, from confined spaces to high-rise construction sites, and be able to adapt to changing conditions and work safely at all times.

WILDLIFE BIOLOGIST

A wildlife biologist is a scientist who studies animals and their habitats, as well as the relationship between humans and the environment. They focus on conservation, research, and management of wildlife populations and their natural ecosystems.

Wildlife biologists play an important role in understanding the behaviors and needs of wildlife species. They collect data on animals, such as population size, distribution, and behavior, as well as their interactions with their environment. Through their research, they gain knowledge of the environmental factors that impact the health and survival of these animals, such as climate change, pollution, and habitat loss.

Wildlife biologists use their findings to develop and implement conservation and management plans to protect wildlife species and their habitats. They may work for government agencies, non-profit organizations, or research institutions, and collaborate with other biologists, landowners, and local communities to achieve conservation goals.

In addition to research and conservation efforts, wildlife biologists also work on resolving conflicts between humans and wildlife. They may help develop programs to prevent damage to crops, manage invasive species, or provide education and outreach to local communities about the importance of wildlife conservation.

To become a wildlife biologist, a strong foundation in science and mathematics is essential. This includes completing a bachelor's degree in biology, ecology, or a related field, as well as pursuing graduate-level coursework in wildlife biology or conservation biology. Many wildlife biologists also gain practical experience through internships or fieldwork, which may involve monitoring wildlife populations, collecting data, and working with other scientists and field researchers.

Due to the nature of their work, wildlife biologists often spend time outdoors, collecting data and observing wildlife in their natural habitats. This may involve hiking through forests, studying animal behavior, or working with landowners to manage wildlife populations.

Overall, the work of a wildlife biologist is critical for understanding and protecting our natural environment. They play a vital role in conserving wildlife populations, preserving ecosystems, and ensuring that we maintain a healthy balance between humans and the natural world.

WINE SOMMELIER

Wine sommeliers are professionals who specialize in the study, selection, and service of wine. They are experts in all things wine-related, from the grape varieties and winemaking processes to the nuances of taste and pairing with food. Wine sommeliers work in a variety of settings, including restaurants, hotels, wine bars, and wineries.

To become a wine sommelier, one typically completes extensive training and certification. The Wine & Spirit Education Trust (WSET) and the Court of Master Sommeliers are two of the most prestigious organizations that offer certifications for aspiring wine professionals. These certifications require a deep understanding of wine theory, tasting technique, and industry knowledge.

In a restaurant setting, a wine sommelier is responsible for managing the wine program, curating the wine list, and ensuring that each guest's wine experience is top-notch. They work closely with the chef to develop food and wine pairings that complement each other and enhance the overall dining experience. They must also have an in-depth knowledge of the restaurant's menu, so they can recommend the perfect wine to go with each dish.

Sommeliers must be able to make recommendations to guests with a variety of preferences and budgets. They must also have excellent communication skills to explain the nuances of the wine to the guest in an approachable and informative manner. They are responsible for maintaining the restaurant's wine inventory, ensuring that wines are stored properly, and making sure that wines are served at the correct temperature.

In addition to working in restaurants, wine sommeliers can also work for wine distributors or importers. In this capacity, they are responsible for selecting and importing wines from around the world to sell to restaurants and wine shops. They must have a deep understanding of the wine market and be able to predict which wines will sell well in a particular region.

Sommeliers also play an important role in the wine industry as educators. They may teach wine classes, lead wine tastings, or speak at wine events to share their knowledge with others. Some may also write about wine or consult with wineries on the production and marketing of their wines.

One of the most important skills for a wine sommelier is the ability to taste and evaluate wine. They must be able to identify the various characteristics of wine, including the grape variety, the vintage, and the region it was produced. They must also be able to detect subtle aromas and flavors that are specific to each wine. This takes extensive training and experience, as well as passion and a natural talent for tasting.

WRITER

A writer is someone who uses the power of words to communicate, entertain, and inform. Writing is an art form that is used in countless different mediums, including books, magazines, newspapers, blogs, social media, film and television scripts, and many more. Writers are responsible for creating the stories, articles, essays, or any other content that we read or watch. They use their imagination, skill, and creativity to craft compelling stories and make us laugh, cry, or think.

Writing is a craft that can take many different forms. Writers can specialize in fiction or non-fiction, poetry or prose, journalism or screenplays. They can also specialize in different genres, such as romance, mystery, science fiction, or historical fiction. Regardless of the type of writing they specialize in, all writers share a common goal: to create something that is both interesting and informative.

Writers must have a strong command of language, grammar, and style. They must be able to express their ideas clearly and effectively, using the right words to convey their message. Good writers are also great observers of the world around them, constantly taking in new information and using it to inform their writing. They have a deep understanding of the human condition and the way that people think and behave, which they use to create believable and relatable characters.

To be a successful writer, one must be disciplined and focused. Writing is not always easy, and it often requires long hours of hard work and a great deal of self-discipline. Writers must be able to overcome writer's block, push through periods of low creativity, and stay motivated even when the work is tough.

One of the key skills a writer must possess is the ability to research effectively. Whether writing fiction or non-fiction, writers must be able to find and use credible sources of information to support their work. This requires strong research skills, as well as a deep understanding of how to use and analyze data.

Another important skill for writers is the ability to work collaboratively. Many writers work on teams with editors, designers, and other creative professionals. They must be able to communicate effectively with these colleagues, as well as accept constructive feedback and incorporate it into their work.

In today's digital age, writers must also have an understanding of how to write for the web. This means understanding search engine optimization, knowing how to write headlines and summaries that grab the reader's attention, and being able to write content that is easily scannable and digestible.

YOGA INSTRUCTOR

A yoga teacher is a trained professional who teaches individuals or groups of people the practice of yoga. The role of a yoga teacher is to guide and facilitate their students in the practice of yoga asana, pranayama, meditation, and other related practices that promote physical, mental, and spiritual well-being.

To become a yoga teacher, one must undergo extensive training, which includes learning yoga philosophy, anatomy, and alignment. They also need to learn how to create a safe and inclusive environment for all individuals, regardless of their level of experience or physical abilities.

The practice of yoga is more than just a physical exercise, it is a way of life. A yoga teacher not only instructs students on how to do the poses correctly, but also guides them through the deeper aspects of yoga such as mindfulness, meditation, and breathwork.

The typical day of a yoga teacher starts with planning the class. This involves choosing the asanas that are appropriate for the students' level, preparing any props that are required, and deciding on the flow of the class. During the class, the teacher guides students through the poses, provides cues on alignment, and offers modifications for those who need them.

Yoga teachers also need to be skilled at adapting to the needs of their students. They must be able to create classes that are appropriate for different ages, levels of experience, and physical abilities. A skilled yoga teacher can help students work through injuries or limitations, and provide options for them to participate fully in the class.

In addition to teaching classes, yoga teachers may also offer private lessons or work with individuals one-on-one to develop personalized yoga programs. They may also lead retreats that focus on specific aspects of yoga practice, such as meditation or pranayama.

To be a successful yoga teacher, one must also possess excellent communication skills. A yoga teacher must be able to clearly explain instructions and provide feedback to their students in a way that is understandable and supportive. Additionally, a yoga teacher must have a strong ability to connect with their students on a personal level, understanding their unique needs and helping them to achieve their goals.

Finally, a yoga teacher must also be passionate about their work. The role of a yoga teacher is to help students find inner peace, balance, and well-being. This requires a deep commitment to the practice of yoga and a desire to share that knowledge and experience with others.

WATCHMAKER

Watchmaking is the art and science of crafting, assembling, and repairing watches and clocks. A watchmaker is a skilled craftsman who designs, assembles, and repairs watches and timepieces. They are experts in precision engineering and work with the tiniest of parts to create intricate and complex mechanisms that keep time accurate to the second.

The history of watchmaking dates back centuries, with the earliest mechanical clocks being developed in Europe during the 14th century. As watchmaking technology evolved, so did the craftsmanship required to make these precision instruments. Today, watchmakers still utilize many traditional techniques, but also incorporate modern technology to create timepieces that are both reliable and aesthetically pleasing.

One of the primary responsibilities of a watchmaker is to assemble and repair watches. This involves working with a wide range of components, from tiny screws and gears to delicate hairsprings and balance wheels. They use a variety of specialized tools and machines to measure, test, and adjust the various components to ensure accuracy and precision in timekeeping.

A watchmaker typically works in a clean, quiet workshop or studio, often working alone or with a small team of other skilled craftsmen. They may also work for a watch manufacturer or a jewelry store that specializes in high-end timepieces. In addition to their technical skills, watchmakers must also have an eye for design and aesthetics, as the beauty and style of a watch are just as important as its functionality.

One of the most fascinating aspects of watchmaking is the attention to detail required. A watchmaker must be extremely precise and patient, with the ability to work with tiny components and adjust them to within fractions of a millimeter. They use specialized tools, such as loupes and magnifying glasses, to inspect and work with the smallest parts of a watch.

In addition to assembly and repair, watchmakers also design and create their own timepieces. This involves creating detailed sketches and plans, selecting materials, and designing and building the mechanisms that power the watch. A watchmaker must have a thorough understanding of the physics and engineering behind how watches work, as well as an artistic eye for creating a watch that is visually stunning and unique.

In conclusion, a watchmaker is a skilled craftsman who designs, assembles, and repairs watches and timepieces. They must have a thorough understanding of the engineering and physics behind how watches work, as well as an artistic eye for creating a watch that is visually stunning and unique.

ZOOLOGIST

A zoologist is a professional who studies and works with animals, both in the wild and in captivity. Their work involves observing animal behavior, conducting experiments, collecting and analyzing data, and making recommendations for the conservation and management of animal populations. Zoologists may work in a variety of settings, including research laboratories, zoos, aquariums, and natural habitats.

Zoologists have a passion for animals and a deep interest in understanding their behavior, biology, and ecology. They are responsible for researching and studying a wide range of animal species, from tiny insects to large mammals, and everything in between. Zoologists are fascinated by the complexities of the animal kingdom and are dedicated to advancing scientific knowledge to better understand the world around us.

One of the primary duties of a zoologist is to study the behavior of animals in their natural habitats. This may involve observing and recording animal behavior, tracking animal movements and migration patterns, and analyzing data to gain insights into the lives and habits of different species. By understanding the behavior of animals, zoologists can better predict their movements and patterns, which is essential for managing and conserving wildlife populations.

In addition to studying the behavior of animals in the wild, zoologists also work with animals in captivity, such as those found in zoos, aquariums, and research facilities. Zoologists are responsible for ensuring the welfare and safety of captive animals, developing and implementing enrichment programs to keep animals mentally and physically stimulated, and ensuring that animals receive appropriate medical care.

Zoologists may also be involved in research that helps to develop conservation strategies for endangered species. This may involve studying the genetic makeup of different populations, analyzing the environmental factors that impact the survival of different species, and developing strategies for habitat restoration and protection. Zoologists also work with government agencies and nonprofit organizations to develop and implement conservation plans that help to protect wildlife and their habitats.

Another important aspect of a zoologist's job is education and public outreach. Zoologists are often involved in teaching and educating the public about the importance of conservation and the need to protect endangered species. They may give talks, lead tours of zoos and aquariums, and participate in community outreach programs to promote environmental education and awareness.

Made in United States
Troutdale, OR
11/08/2023

14388930R00115